...SPELL
21:08:09
Stuart Broad's 5/37 at the Brit Oval

The spell that decided the Ashes. Less than two weeks before, England had lost the fourth Test by an innings within two-and-a-half days. Just a week before, the nationwide cry of "sack the lot of them" was still in full flow. Broad himself was deemed to be one of those facing the axe. And then… this. Broad came on at the Brit Oval with the Aussies 66/0 and looking serene. (Pundits, don't forget, had declared England's first innings 332 as below par.) Broad's first ball was over-pitched and driven to the boundary for four by Simon Katich. But with the last ball of that first over, Shane Watson was trapped leg-before. Soon Broad was bamboozling Ricky Ponting with his late movement from good-length balls, eventually enticing the Aussie skipper to play onto his stumps. Mike Hussey was late on another full-length ball that moved back late, Clarke fell to a sharp catch by Trott at short cover and Broad had four wickets for eight runs from 21 balls. Sensational. Next, Broad clean bowled Brad Haddin, swiping across one, and Australia were 111/7 and in the cart.

THIS YEAR'S BIGGEST...

...STORM IN A TEACUP
13:05:09
Chris Gayle speaks his mind

So, out of the goodness of your heart, you've walked away from a job that pays £140k a week in a nice, warm-ish climate to come and – effectively – lead an Arctic expedition for a fraction of the reward. And people keep saying you should have done it sooner. Eventually you're going to crack.

We're talking about Windies skipper Chris Gayle, who arrived on the eve of the ill-scheduled England-West Test series in May after staying longer than originally planned at the IPL. Gayle finally cracked in a phone interview with the *Guardian*: he didn't exactly rage against his critics; it was more a kind of mumbled grumble, as he warned Andrew Strauss to "stay out of people's business... Focus on his team, don't worry about West Indies, don't worry about me. Tell him don't sleep with Chris on his mind; tell him get Chris off his mind."

Gayle added that if T20 replaced Tests, he "wouldn't be so sad" but that Strauss might be because "there is no way he can make the change. So tough luck."

As for the Windies' captaincy, "It's definitely not something I'm looking to hang on to. I need some time for myself, to be honest with you." Churchillian it wasn't. And, within months, Gayle and the rest of the Windies' first team were on strike over pay and contracts.

...TURNING-POINT
13:06:09
Shahid Afridi's T20 catch

How bad were Pakistan in their first game at the ICC World Twenty20? Well, they lost to England with a display in the field that was so bad that skipper Younus Khan was reduced to grinning and shaking his head, forlornly. And then they wound up winning the tournament, exactly two weeks later. The turning-point? Possibly the game against New Zealand at the Oval. Umar Gul would go on to take five wickets for six runs – the best-ever bowling in Twenty20 – but the pivotal point came in his first over. Gul's first scalp, Scott Styris, fell to a brilliant running-back-to-the-boundary catch from Shahid Afridi. The catch – and Afridi's look-at-me celebration in front of the fans – was possibly the moment of the tournament and the moment that inspired Pakistan from Keystone Copsery to new heights. The Kiwis were blown away for 99. Pakistan passed them with 41 balls to spare. And went on to become champions.

...CLIFFHANGER
12:07:09
Monty and Jimmy bat out at Cardiff

We all doubted whether the 2009 Ashes could really live up to the heart-stopping dramas of 2005. But on the last day of the first Test at Cardiff, we had a finish to rival anything from four years previously. In fact, this was a mirror image of Old Trafford 2005, when the last Aussie pair, Brett Lee and Glenn McGrath, had clung on against the odds as England pushed for victory. Here, England – who had been, frankly, outclassed – came into the last day headed for defeat. Paul Collingwood (74 from 245 balls) did the graft, batting for nearly six hours and ragging England back from 70/5 before lunch and 169/7 at tea – but it all seemed in vain when he finally, meekly, surrendered to Peter Siddle in the last hour, ninth out with England still six runs behind. But last-wicket pair Jimmy Anderson and Monty Panesar resisted for the last 69 deliveries of the match to salvage the draw, with a little help from some time-wasting antics. Punter Ponting called those "pretty ordinary" in the press conference afterwards. Where on his Ordinaryometer Punter put the failure of the best bowlers in Australia to remove Monty Panesar (Monty Panesar!) in 35 balls over a 37-minute period was not discussed.

...FIASCO
07:01:09
KP-Moorogate

The first week of the new year and whatever resolutions England supremo Hugh Morris might have had went up in smoke as the row between captain KP and coach Peter Moores spilled out into the public domain, filling the papers and airwaves for a week. In short: KP didn't think England could win the Ashes with Mooro as coach. Mooro didn't want to go. Rumours spread all week: had the ECB sounded out the players and found them divided in their loyalties? Did Flintoff want Moores to stay and KP to go? Had KP had several meetings with the ECB top brass re: potential new coaches, before the top brass decided the skipper shouldn't have quite so much say? With KP, weirdly, on safari for the week, the story snowballed until, on Day 8, the ECB called a press conference, made the journalists wait for four hours and gave a one-minute statement to the effect that coach and captain had both left their jobs. Soon, Andrew Strauss was confirmed as the man to knock things back into shape, which turned out okay.

...EMBARRASSMENT
07:02:09
England bowled out for 51 in Jamaica

We are living in an era deemed to be the age of the batsman. England don't seem to have got that particular memo. The nadir came at Sabina Park. West Indies had won just two Tests in 30 ahead of the series, Andrew Strauss' first in charge. But Jerome Taylor's 5/11 skittled England for 51 to wrap up an innings victory, as the tourists failed to make a winning start to a series for the 14th consecutive rubber. Just one of those days for England? Well, it was the fifth time in 15 months that they had been bowled out for less than 111. In December 2007, they were all out for 81 against Sri Lanka in Galle; in the very next Test, against New Zealand at Hamilton, they were skittled for 110; at Stanford, they were bowled out for 99 by the Superstars; at a warm-up game in India 10 days later, they were bowled out for 98 and then, in the fourth Ashes Test at Leeds in August, England's best batsmen were all out for 102 inside 34 overs. So... work still to do.

...INSPIRATION
12:06:09
Pakistan and Sri Lanka line up at Lord's

The Cricket Circus just keeps on going. "Crucial" series are talked up; middle-aged men make their living asking young men about how their groin strains are progressing. But sometimes real life really does intrude on our game – and never more dramatically and – genuinely – tragically – than in February when terrorists attacked the Sri Lankan team on the way to their Test match against Pakistan at the Gaddafi Stadium in Lahore. Five security officers lost their lives when the Sirils' motorcade came under ambush from 12 gunmen within sight of the stadium. Several members of the Sri Lankan party were injured, though – remarkably – no-one was killed. The incident certainly put paid to teams wanting to visit Pakistan for the foreseeable future – and, on the heels of the Mumbai attacks, could have closed down international cricket more widely. Fast-forward to Lord's in June: Sri Lanka and Pakistan line up together for the World Twenty20 for the first time since the attack. You could have forgiven the Sirils for calling it a day. That they had carried on and taken their part in cricket's biggest international celebration was braver and more significant than many observers noticed.

...TALKING-POINT
22:09:09
Lily Allen on Test Match Special

TMS has been at the peak of its game this year: the Henry Blofeld-Phil Tufnell double act was better than anyone could ever have predicted, Geoff Boycott remains must-hear broadcasting and the peerless Agnew held it all together. And then there was Lily Allen, a lunchtime guest on the third day of the final Test. The appearance of anyone under 60 on TMS always incites idiots to come out of the woodwork. Someone wrote into the BBC TMS blog to say that TMS shouldn't have people like Lily Allen on it. What? Women? People with a bit of character about them? Or – surely not! – people who've been to posh schools. (Imagine that.) The faux-chav pop minx said she'd like to see the Ashes played over nine Tests ("all-out war") and championed the "long slog" of Test cricket over Twenty20, with Aggers suddenly sounding rather headmasterly. Sure there were cringy moments but no more than when the View From the Boundary slot includes A.N. Other actor struggling to remember some tiresome details from his trip to Headingley in 1958.

...HOT POTATO
17.02.09
Sir Allen Stanford

The announcement that US authorities were investigating Sir Allen Stanford, at that stage still the ECB's partner for a series of megabucks Twenty20 games, over an alleged $8billion fraud sent shockwaves through cricket. Well, ish: in fact, most commentators declared that they weren't surprised one bit. All the previously stated cases against him – owning helicopter/moustache, preferring T20 to Test cricket, being American and "vulgar" – were conflated into I-told-you-sos. Stanford's disappearance when the allegations became public didn't look good – it looked, let's be honest, comical – and soon the ECB was severing ties. Kevin Pietersen's *News of the World* column summed up English cricket's confused approach. The Texan was a "sleazebag", said KP, while bemoaning the money he had lost on ripped-up personal contracts with the man. Whether KP thought Stanford was a sleazebag at the point he signed the contracts was unclear.

UNHAPPY BIRTHDAY?

WHY YOUR D.O.B COULD STOP YOU GOING TO THE TOP

SEPTEMBER-OCTOBER 85 PLAYERS

NOVEMBER-DECEMBER 49

JANUARY-FEBRUARY 45

MARCH-APRIL 50

MAY-JUNE 39

JULY-AUGUST 31

Birthdays of English-born, English-qualified county cricketers, 2008 season

You are nearly three times as likely to win a professional cricket contract if you were born in September or October than if you were born in July or August.

Coincidence? Probably not: the theory is that children who are the oldest in their year at school can gain sporting advantages at an early age and hold onto them for life. When an under-nine team is selected, the bigger, more physically developed children are likely to get chosen; these are likely to be those among the oldest in the year.

A child born in August will be almost 12 months younger than one born in September. That makes a big difference when you're nine or ten. By the time you're 15 or 16 or 20 or 21, it makes no difference at all. But by that stage, the children picked out early as high achievers have had years of better coaching, properly focused practice and playing the other "elite" children.

It's a phenomenon that has been documented in other sports: in American pro baseball, there are 62 per cent more players born in August than in July (the cut-off for age-group teams in the US is August 1, as opposed to September 1 in the UK).

JONATHAN AGNEW

The BBC's voice of cricket on people dressed as bears and not making a boob of himself

I was packed off to boarding school when I was about eight, so I've always been an itinerant sort of person. If anything it makes you appreciate being at home more.

Behind the microphone, you become a caricature of yourself. A lot of journos have eight hours to mull over their opinions. But for me when something happens – bang! I'm on BBC 5. That's the real test. You get a great kick out of that, but you're also up there to make a big boob.

There's too much cricket. Full stop. Test Match Special? I wonder how many Test matches really do feel special these days. There's just too much of it.

Elton John was absolutely incredible as a lunchtime guest on TMS. I've probably listened to his music more than anyone else's in my life. I was terrified. But he was incredible, he just never drew breath. He just clearly sits and watches the game on some big plasma screen all day. He had been watching West Indies v Zimbabwe in an ODI that very day!

I don't have the appetite to watch a full day's county cricket. A Test match is just such an intense six days in my case. Although it is great fun and each day is different, the long hours of a Test wear me out. You need time to build yourself up to begin again for the next one.

I never run out of things to say. But I did run out of questions for Edward Fox once, in a half-hour stint in which he didn't seem interested at all. My last question was, "What do you think of the euro"? That happens.

The ECB wants people dressed up as bears, and wants to appeal to eight-year-olds. But that's wrong: you need to appeal to the parents – they're the ones who bring the kids along. Same with TMS.

Our audience is regenerating. We get stacks of emails from students, girls and boys: it's because we appeal to the right level of intellect and age. The other day, the controller of FiveLive had an email from an 11-year-old called Gemma, who said the programme was "wicked".

Sky's coverage is slick, it's colourful, it's interesting and they've proved they are thoroughly committed to covering cricket. But the shame is that the audience remains too small for cricket's well-being. Whether we like it or not, there are plenty of people out there who would prefer to spend £40 a month on something else.

The last thing I want to do when I get home is talk very much.

Johnners [Brian Johnston] was the chocolate cake fan. I'm a fruit cake man and listeners have generally made the switch. We get some excellent fruit cakes and Blowers [Henry Blofeld] seems to be satisfied with the wine and general alcoholic beverages that get sent in. People might think it's ridiculous, but it's all about the interaction with the listeners. TMS has always been a programme that has touched people. If thanking Mrs Snookes for her chocolate cake is one way of making people think there are people out there and we're all one big happy family, then that's what it's all about. That's what we are trying to preserve.

It's hard as nails!

PAUL COLLINGWOOD
BINGO

'He's made the most of his limited ability'	'The young lad Collingwood'* * No points if Nasser says this	'Nudger'/ 'nurdler'/ 'Dibbly'/ 'dobbly'
Coded class-war comparison with Alastair Cook	Beefy saying semi-amusedly: 'Well, Duncan Fletcher says he can bowl at 85 mph!'	Anything that could also be said of '60s kitchen sink drama eg 'gritty', 'hard', 'tough', 'cinematic social realism'
'Very popular in the dressing room'	'Unsung'/ 'Scrapper'/ 'unsung scrapper'	'You don't take a single to Collingwood!'

How to play
1) Don flat cap
2) Listen to radio/TV or read your morning paper
3) Tick off the phrases as they come up
4) Don't write in if you get them all! We don't care!

ANDREW STRAUSS

The elevation to the captaincy didn't stop Andrew Strauss scoring runs – in fact, quite the opposite. Strauss was England's leading run scorer both in the West Indies and, at home, as they reclaimed the Ashes. Here, we look at Strauss' 142 in Barbados in February compared to his 108 in Chennai in December.

What is interesting about the Barbados innings is how quickly it was scored: from 210 balls, a strike rate of 67.61. The Chennai ton was scored at a strike rate of 44.26

Graphic 1 shows a breakdown of whether Strauss chose to attack (blue), defend (red) or leave alone (yellow) balls during his Barbados century; while **Graphic 2** is the same breakdown for the Chennai innings. What is noticeable is the increased number of balls wide outside off stump that Strauss attacked in the West Indies, on a line that he was content to leave or defend in India.

It's clear Strauss approached his Barbados innings with a more positive mindset – even a conscious effort to attack from the front. On returning to the side in 2008, Strauss had cut out "risky" shots and adopted a more stolid style than previously. The series

since had yielded strike-rates of 45, 44, 38 and 44. But in the first three Tests of his new tenure as captain, his strike rate went up to 58 – and that's probably not a coincidence.

It wasn't just Strauss' scoring rate that has changed. His more attacking approach saw him score in regions not previously featured in his wagon wheels. **Graphic 3** – from Barbados – reveals a well-rounded wheel, with shots all around the wicket, though the left-hander's penchant for scoring behind the wicket on the offside is still clear: eight of his 18 boundaries (blue) were scored through that region.

Compare that to **Graphic 4**, a wagon wheel of his second-innings hundred at Chennai: note that here Strauss scored virtually no runs straight down the ground.

In Barbados, Strauss was happy to score straight down the ground, with a roster of on-drives, and even brought up his 100 with a six (red) off Sulieman Benn. In the past – particularly during the 2006/07 Ashes – opponents have tied up Strauss by starving him of the wide balls he prefers to score from. These days, applying that strategy would be far less successful.

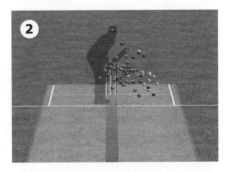

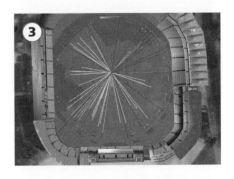

"In the past opponents have tied up Strauss by starving him of the wide balls he prefers to score from"

SHOT 5: SIX!

RS Well, he's got the licence here to go for the Full Monty. Six out of six. This is a pressure ball for Broad. If this goes out of the ground, then that team meeting might just be extended a little more.

DL Eight deliveries to go. It's 195/3. We were speculating on 200. They're WAY past 200.

RS All because of this gigantic over. Still not completed. Back to over the wicket. It's a scrambled brain as far as Broad is concerned out there.

DL This is a crowd warning! Look out!

Broad bowls a half-volley, 79.5 mph on middle-and-off. Down on one knee, Yuvraj hoists it over mid-wicket

RS Five! Yessssss! Thirty! With one ball to go! Can he make it six out of six?

DL Well, it's show-time here. Would you believe this? Clean as you like, here he goes again! Yuvraj Singh: 44. 11 deliveries.

Collingwood on the boundary, looking anxious

SHOT 6: SIX!

RS We saw Herschelle Gibbs doing it in a game against Holland in the World Cup. It's never happened in TT cricket. There's every chance now. Yuvraj must be favourite here to put the sixth one into the crowd as well. Kingsmead on its feet, so is the commentary box. Here goes Broad. Last ball...

Leg-side half-volley, 78.5 mph. Yuvraj onto one knee again and puts this one over square leg as well

And he's put it away! Or has he? Yes – into the crowd! Six sixes in an over!

SHOT 2: SIX!

Full-length ball, 80 mph, on middle-stump. Flicked effortlessly over square leg

RS Six more! Just a flick of the wrists and away she goes into the crowd. Magnificent hitting from the left-hander!

DL Magnificent hitting this. Just a flick, nothing more. Hard hat time. Look out in the crowd.

RS Well, this was a new ball taken: the first one is lying somewhere in the road outside Kingsmead. The second one flicked into the crowd.

TV cameras cut to Flintoff shaking his head and looking rueful on the rope

DL 26 from 8 deliveries, Yuvraj. He's not got his eye in yet.

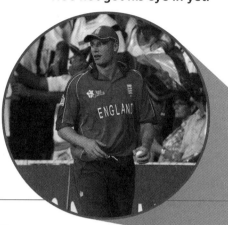

SHOT 1: SIX!

Ravi Shastri Now, Broad into his final over. A few words exchanged between Yuvraj and Flintoff...

Yuvraj picks up a 78-mph slower length ball from off-stump and hoists it over deep mid-wicket

That's huge. That is a biggie, it's out of here!

David Lloyd Ravi, I'm backing this one. I think this is one of the biggest. Into orbit.

RS Well, 111 metres is the longest, but this might go the distance. I think those few words with Flintoff just charged him up a bit. That was a magnificent strike. Crunching sound as ball hit willow. Now a man drops down to deep mid-wicket. Third man comes up. Yuvraj has seen that. He's got a wide range of shots: what's he going to do?

Broad stands at back of his run, licking his lips and looking slightly reluctant

RS Now, around the wicket. Will it make a difference?

High full-toss outside off-stump, 80.8 mph. Yuvraj depatches it over backward point

It doesn't! It's four in a row! 24 off the first four balls!

DL Here it is again! Yuvraj Singh: 38 from 10 deliveries. England are having a conference meeting. They're in bits!

Collingwood strides over from mid-off to offer Broad some advice.

YUVRAJ SINGH'S SIX SIXES
ENGLAND v INDIA 19:09:07 KINGSMEAD

Yuvraj Singh hitting Stuart Broad for 36 in an over, as seen by David Lloyd and Ravi Shastri in the ESPN gantry

SHOT 3: SIX!

Off-stump 79.3-mph half-volley from Broad. Yuvraj steps away and hits him over extra-cover

RS This is in the air again! It clears long-on! Three in a row! Yuvraj is doing to Broad what Mascarenhas did to him at the Oval.

DL It's raining sixes here at Kingsmead! There's another. Look at the technique: right foot out of the way; full swing of the bat. Yuvraj: 32 from nine deliveries.

RS Six! Six! Six! Absolute carnage!

STUART BROAD

England's Ashes hero first made his mark as a 20-year-old T20 champ. When SPIN met him in June 2009, he looked back on his early days, England's T20 struggles and his own rapid progress

Stuart Broad is arguably the first product of cricket's Twenty20 generation. No player before him and not many since had made their international debut on the back of T20 performances. But it was the teenage Broad's part in Leicestershire's triumphant Twenty20 Cup team that first grabbed the attention of the England selectors in 2006. Now, only Paul Collingwood and Kevin Pietersen have played more times for England's Twenty20 side. In 2009, Broad turned down the opportunity to play at the Indian Premier League, insisting he wanted to focus on his duties with England this summer. His decision –

and the selectors' faith in him – was resoundingly vindicated by his Ashes-snatching performance at the Brit Oval in August.

You started your career in a successful Leicestershire Twenty20 team. You have now played 12 times for a not-very-successful England T20 team. What's the difference?
Leicestershire were successful because they had a good plan and each player knew what role they were going to play. I always bowled four overs up front, tried to get a couple of wickets, then we had three spinners who'd come in and tie it down. Darren

Maddy would hit it up front and Paul Nixon in the middle would take the spin apart with his reverse sweeps. Everyone knew what their role was.

You look at the England T20 side and it's hard to say what the side actually is. We've used 43 players with 11 different opening partnerships. It's hard to say "England aren't any good at T20 cricket" because the team has changed so dramatically. England need to settle on a side that they think can move forward. We don't play a huge amount of Twenty20, so it's hard to get a settled role. Forty-three players in 15 games is a lot...

Broad averaged 31 with the bat in Tests: "I've always believed that No 8s should score 100s and I think I still have that ability"

You know all these stats off the top of your head?!

Well, that was only because we had Steve Davies and Amjad Khan making their debuts for England in Trinidad and their shirts had their numbers on. And we were all going, "We can't have used 43 players". When people say, "Oh England don't get off to a good start," it's hard to know exactly who hasn't made a good start because it's been a different opening partnership almost every time.

What did England learn from the first World T20, in 2007?

We'd beaten India in England 4-3 in the NatWest Series and flew out the next day to the World T20 with eight or nine changes to the squad... It didn't work out for us because probably again the game plan and players' roles weren't as clear as they could have been. But it was an eye-opener. It proved we weren't very good at Twenty20 cricket and there's a lot of scope for improvement. We didn't bat anywhere near like anyone else in the tournament. People were getting 170, 180 and we were crawling to 130 and 140 and that's something we still need to work on.

Broad fires for Leicestershire in the 2006 Twenty20 Cup – and catches the selectors' eyes

England were thrashed 5-0 in the ODIs in India in November 2008. When you're on the park, do you sense that India have taken the one-day game to a different level to England?

I don't think it's just England. India went to New Zealand and were scoring 400 and Tendulkar was getting 160... Obviously the IPL has helped them do that: they've learned new shots and new skills and they're a very very dangerous batting line-up. Thats why it's good we've got a few England players who've had a bit of exposure in the IPL, so they can see how it really develops players.

As a bowler, did you pick a bad time to come into international cricket?

That's why I worked on my batting really, so I could have some fun as well! It's a difficult question after last winter where we played on some very turgid wickets and it was easy for

batsmen to get 100s on occasion. I think everyone wants to see a good balance. I remember watching Donald and Atherton in '98 and exciting battles like that: that really got me

intrigued by cricket. No-one wants to see 700 plays 600 declared: it's hard to play in let alone watch. You think back to that '05 Ashes that got the country so loved up to cricket: it was 350 plays 350 and it turned and Warne was in the game: that's what people want to see. Don't get me wrong: we should have wickets that are good for batting but they have to deteriorate in some way.

How high would you like to bat?

Seven or eight is ideal for me. I need to keep working on that. I have a very settled game plan at the moment and I'm very comfortable with that. Which

"Andy Flower changed me as a batsman completely"

is mainly down to Andy Flower. But I've always believed that No 8s in international cricket should have the ability to score 100s and I think I do have that ability in me. Andy Flower changed me as a batsman completely on the New Zealand tour in 2008. He dedicated a lot of his time to helping me develop, which I appreciate a lot. Chatting to him as a left-hander really helped me. I owe a lot to him for that.

TALL STORIES

It's a fact – everyone in cricket is taller than you think. Even Ian Bell. Apart from the little Master, who's quite small

Tony Greig 6ft 7.5
Comm box legend is the tallest-ever England Test player

Michael Vandort 6 ft 5
The Sirils' opener is the tallest in Test cricket

Sulieman Benn 6 ft 7
The West Indies' slow left-armer is the tallest Test spinner

Ian Bell 5 ft 10
Taller than you'd think (one inch taller than UK national average)

Chris Tremlett 6 ft 7
Hot-and-cold Hampshire pace man is the tallest current England player

7'0"	
6'6"	
6'0"	
5'6"	
5'0"	
4'5"	
4'0"	

Does Slinger Malinga REALLY have a new hairdo for every series, as he claims? Yes, readers, he really does. And sometimes two…

THE SHOAIB JUNIOR
June 2004
Australia tour

THE BOUFFANT SPACESHIP
July 2005
West Indies at home

THE COLLEGE BOY
April 2005
New Zealand tour

The Ena Sharples
December 2005,
India tour

THE McENROE
March 2006
Pakistan at home

Bob Willis 6 ft 6
Pace legend-turned-gantry-doom-monger is the tallest Sky pundit

Sachin Tendulkar 5 ft 5
But even the Little Master is an inch taller than ex-Sirils whizz Aravinda de Silva

Will Jefferson 6 ft 10
The Nottinghamshire opener is the tallest current first-class player

Adam Gilchrist 6 ft 1
Tallest record-breaking wicket-keeper of modern era. Probably

Joel Garner 6 ft 8
The Big Bird. So called because he was big and, er, a fast bowler

"IT'S NOT WHAT I ASKED FOR"

THE MACY GRAY
March 2006
Bangladesh tour

BLAME IT ON RIO
May 2006
England tour

THE SIDESHOW BOB
May 2006
England tour (still)

**THE FULL
KEN DODD**
August 2006
South Africa at home

THE LION KING
World Cup, April 2007
Doesn't it get hot under there?

enough said...*

107

Number of years since there has been a new Ashes venue in England – before Cardiff's SWALEC Stadium on July 3

8

Number of English venues that have hosted England-Australia Tests: Sheffield's Bramall Lane hosting just one, in 1902

18

Number of Ashes Tests that had been played at Lord's between England's wins there, in 1934 and 2009.

*figures that speak for themselves

HOW TO BOWL FASTER

By Ian Pont, coach to Darren Gough and Dale Steyn

When bowling, focus on what your non-bowling arm is doing. A lot of cricketers neglect this, but if you want to bowl faster, you need to pay attention to the arm opposite the one with the ball. Assuming you're a right-armer, when you complete your action your left arm should be pointing upwards towards the sky behind you in a straight line. Your left arm needs to do its work.

Think about it: your shoulders are connected. If your left arm and shoulder are pulling you through in the right way, your right arm and shoulder will come with them. Your bowling hand should end up under your armpit as your left arm points behind you. Pulling with your left arm as you bowl gives you 180-degree shoulder rotation – it makes you drive through the ball as you're releasing it.

And remember: your head should be pointing towards the target – not somewhere out towards cover as many people seem to think.

Opinions differ on exactly how to work with your leading arm. Some people like to bend it at the elbow and drive it through and down into their ribs. Dennis Lillee compares the movement to pulling down an old-fashioned toilet chain. But others would argue that method pulls your weight down into the ground, when you're actually trying to drive your weight forward.

Instead, try keeping your left arm straight out in front of you and chopping down like a karate chop until it is behind you. This will pull your right shoulder forward through the action. You'll absolutely fly through the crease – and give yourself plenty of extra speed. Watch Stuart Broad: this is the way he does it.

Commentary BINGO

Nasser using the phrase 'young lad' to describe someone approaching 30 (Extra point if it's Graham Napier, 28).	"He's got hands like buckets!"	Nick Knight saying he's delighted to be here
Bumble saying things in three different ways (eg. "He's a young boy; a young lad; a new player")	★ "Start the car/ launch the pedalo"	"In the early days it was seen as a bit of a hit and giggle"
"Twenty20 is here to stay"	Bumble filling in co-commentator with details of a player's favourite band	Nasser getting noticeably emotional as he uses the phrase: "Fortress Chelmsford"

How to play
1 Listen carefully to your match radio
2 Tick off the phrases as the commentators say them
3 Find something to do AFTER lunch

ANDREW FLINTOFF

Andrew Flintoff has always said that he prefers to be seen as a batsman who bowls. But while some of the stats may support that view – his 5/92 at Lord's in the 2009 Ashes was only his third Test five-for – common sense dictates otherwise. Despite a surprising lack of Test wickets, Flintoff has been England's No 1 stock and shock bowler – the man the captain turns to when a new batsman comes in; and the man he turns to when the batters are well set and he needs some control. The dual role is not necessarily good for a man's knees and ankles. Witness the Sri Lanka Test at Lord's in 2006, when Flintoff, then captain, bowled 51 overs in the second innings.

Here we highlight two career peaks of Flintoff's bowling: the first, his over at Edgbaston in 2005, was seen as the perfect over. It came when Australia, chasing 282, were 47/0 in their second innings. Flintoff bowled Justin Langer second ball through sheer force of personality and then set Ricky Ponting up with a glorious five-card trick.

Graphic 1 is the pitch map of that particular over. All balls were pitched on or around a good length and all on a perfect line, preventing any runs (blue) as Fred reduced the visitors to 48/2 in their pursuit of 282.

Graphic 2 shows the same over. Ball 1 (red) was wide enough outside off to be safely blocked by the left-handed Langer, but the tighter line of Ball 2 (blue) saw Langer play on with an inside edge. The right-handed Ponting survived two optimistic leg-before

shouts (yellow and green), before Fred overstepped to extend the over to seven balls. Ball 7 (light blue) was perfect: a leg cutter on the perfect length extracted a big outside edge from Ponting, which was taken easily by Geraint Jones.

Before the 2005 series Adam Gilchrist had smashed 673 runs @ 61.18 against England, including two centuries, but the Aussie stumper/whacker came unstuck with a return of just 181 runs @ 22.62 in the series. Flintoff worked him out from around the wicket, causing confusion in his footwork and doubts in his mind.

Freddie removed Gilchrist four times in the 2005 series, three times caught and once bowled. The keys to his success were his ability to move the ball both ways – and the angle of attack that came from bowling round the wicket. Take Gilchrist's dismissal in the first innings at Lord's.

Graphic 3 shows the over before Flintoff removed him: Flintoff is bowling from around the wicket, slanting the ball into Gilchrist, curbing his options, especially after the first two deliveries (red and white). Getting plenty of bounce from round the wicket, Flintoff gave Gilchrist no width, digging the ball into his ribs and frustrating his natural aggression.

Graphic 4 shows how Flintoff removed him – offering a wide ball (red) followed by a ball that came back in, catching Gilly unawares and forcing him to edge the ball to Geraint Jones.

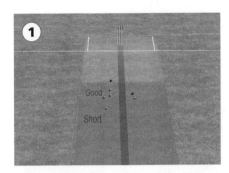

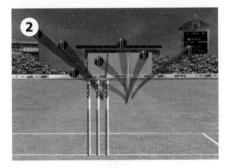

Rajasthan Royals spent the least money of all the eight Indian Premier League franchises at the first IPL auction in February 2008. But the only British-owned team in the IPL invested their cash wisely, with Shane Warne as captain-coach and a roster of canny Twenty20 signings. While other squads seemed to have been picked out of an (expensive) hat, the Royals squad was chosen with a sharply focused view to winning the competition.

Warne, the only non-Indian captain, never had a full-time go at being Australia skipper, but in India, in the game's newest tournament, he proved his mettle against the world's biggest players. Easy to forget now, but before the tournament there were plenty of sceptics who doubted whether made-up all-star teams with no tradition

Shane Warne (captain/coach)
In 20 years of first-class cricket I have never experienced such intensity and passion. The only thing that came close was the Ashes in 2005. Mate, it is so hard to accurately explain what it was like. I mean we had 20,000 people with their faces painted in the colours of the Rajasthan Royals outside the ground on the day of the final. They banged on our bus when we arrived at the ground, "Go the Royals", they were so into it.

The beauty of the IPL was I was bowling to Ganguly in Rajasthan and the crowd were all supporting me, and went berserk when I knocked him over. Nothing compares to it.

My approach as captain and coach was, "Express yourself and be laid

RAJASTHAN ROYALS' IPL WIN

RAJASTHAN ROYALS v CHENNAI SUPER KINGS 01:06:08 MUMBAI

Shane Warne's canny outsiders win the first IPL on a shoestring budget. Warne and coach Jeremy Snape recall building their T20 champs from scratch

could capture the imagination of supporters and TV audiences. The IPL had apparently been thrown together at short notice – in response to the unofficial Indian Cricket League – and had not shaken off the idea that it might be a retirement home for old superstars looking to eke out some extra shekels from their fading careers.

As it turned out, the sceptics were proved wrong. An estimated 100 million Indians tuned in to watch at least some part of the tournament in person or on the television.

With Warne's team taking the title, the BCCI had the perfect result for the inaugural competition: a legend of the game operating at the peak of his powers to bond a mix of youngsters and established stars, to show that cricketing nous counted for more than randomly strewn cash. The Royals topped the group table with 11 wins

from 14 games. In the semi-final, Shane Watson hit 52 and then took 3/10 to inspire a massive 105-run win over Delhi Daredevils, taking the final with the final ball.

In the final, India's spinning all-rounder Yusuf Pathan was the hero: his 3/22 kept MS Dhoni's Chennai Super Kings down to 163/5 – and Pathan's 56 off 39 balls anchored the chase, too, before the Royals won – off the final ball, naturally.

back." That's it. It was only me and a couple of assistants. We didn't have any computers helping us.

I made it as simple as possible. It was old school, mate. We sat around the pool with a beer or a Coke and just talked about cricket. There were no big warm-ups, we swam in the pool, jumped on the bus, tossed a coin and said, "We're batting." We didn't arrive at the ground two hours early, or any of that rubbish.

Royals' mix of young Indians and stars including tournament MVP Shane Watson (fourth right) stormed the inaugural IPL

Jeremy Snape (assistant coach)
We knew we had to pull together very quickly. The first thing to consider was the social chemistry of the dressing-room: three Pakistani legends, a couple of Aussie legends, English coach, Aussie coach, lots of young Indians and a couple of Indian internationals – it was quite a varied mix. So we spent a lot of time trying to get the boys together as quickly as we could because we knew that would impact on the pitch.

The thing you look out for first is the differences in the group. Culturally, some guys are going off to temples to pray, other guys are going off to the pub. Then it's about finding the similarities and shining a light as brightly as possible on those.

The standard of the cricket was very high. Take the best of English Twenty20 cricket, put in four world-class overseas professionals and a crowd of 40,000 and you've got a pretty good product. The cricket was outstanding. There was some amazing Indian young talent, mixed with some world-class performers.

That was one of the great things for me: seeing the youngsters who've hardly played any first-class cricket sitting in the dressing-room just chatting with Younus Khan, Graeme Smith and of course Warney. The melting pot of information and tactics was definitely bubbling out there, and I'm sure English guys will learn a lot when they start playing more in the IPL in the years to come.

Warne: "We didn't arrive at the ground two hours early or any of that rubbish"

10 WAYS TO IMPROVE CRICKET

by **SPIN**'s George Dobell

1. Stop coming off for rain all the time

When you hear the word "dangerous" what do you think? About shark-infested waters and burning buildings, perhaps? Or maybe a weekend in Helmand Province?

What you probably don't think about is damp grass. Or dew. Or some clouds. Because only in cricket are these things considered dangerous.

How often have you seen a game ruined by players fleeing a few spots of rain as if it were poison gas? Or delaying the start due to damp patches so insignificant that you would think nothing of children running around in them? And then, when it's deemed too dangerous to play cricket, coming out and playing football instead. How annoying is that?

So, change number one, would be that games should continue through rain and bad light. Not hurricanes, blizzards or eclipses, clearly, but certainly through drizzle and some cloud cover. The game isn't popular enough that it can alienate those who have paid to come and any change in atmospheric conditions should just be accepted as part and parcel of the game. It is a spectator sport, after all.

2. Stop moaning about playing too much

Charge players with bringing the game into disrepute if they do. Yes, we know they sometimes have to bowl eight overs in a row and stand out in the sun for two hours at a time with nothing but a team of coaches, physios, psychologists and drinks waiters to support them, but they'd do well to remember that other people have to go to work, too. And no-one else gets to put their feet up if it rains, or go warm-weather training each winter, or have a rub down every couple of hours.

Playing cricket for a living remains a wonderful and enviable job.

3. Take the politics out of umpiring

Although the ICC have an elite panel of umpires, there's nothing elite about some of the umpires on there. So, instead of having neutral umpires, the ICC should simply select the best. If all the good ones happen to be Indian, English or Australian, then so be it.

5. Make Andy Flower a football-style England manager

Who picks the England team? Is it Geoff Miller, the National Selector? Or Andy Flower, the team director? Or is it the captain, Andrew Strauss? Or perhaps the managing director, Hugh Morris? And how about Ashley Giles and James Whitaker; where do they fit in?

It's a muddle, isn't it? Who knows who is in charge. What happens when there is a disagreement? And until everyone knows, how can anyone take responsibility?

The solution is to give the coach – or team director – absolute control. Let Flower select the captain, the team and the backroom staff. All the other positions are unnecessary.

4. Make the lbw law more bowler-friendly

Imagine you bowl a perfect off-break or an in-swinger that pitches a foot outside off-stump, nips in and takes the middle stump. Great bowling. So why isn't it great bowling if the batsman manages to get his pad in the way of the ball?

At the moment, batsmen can't be given out if the ball hits them outside the line and they are playing a shot, even if it's going on to hit the stumps. To reward bowlers, encourage batsmen to use their bats. Furthermore, to prevent dull cricket, the LBW law should be amended so that batsmen can be given out even if they are hit outside the line, so long as the umpire considers that the ball is going on to hit the stumps.

6. Get cricket on proper TV

Remind the BBC that they are given almost £3 billion a year by license-fee payers. It might be nice if they could broadcast some shows that don't involve buying, selling or decorating houses. Maybe even some sport. Apart from Formula 1.

7. Make the calendar simple

Sometimes it seems the counties don't actually want anyone to watch them. As if it's not hard enough to follow which day of the week they play, they've now started messing with the start times. So, the next suggestion is that they regulate the fixture programme. Allow Championship cricket to be played from Monday to Thursday, a T20 league on Friday nights and another limited-overs competition – be it 40 or 50 overs a side – on Sunday afternoons. Saturdays might then be the day for a knockout tournament…

8. Bring back the "FA Cup of cricket"

The old C&G Trophy (previously the NatWest or Gillette Cup) remains a much-missed competition and, played as a T20 knockout, could prove successful again. Include Holland, Scotland, Ireland and the minor counties. And give the broadcasting rights to a "free to view" channel.

9. Get the Indian Premier League under control

Is the IPL good for cricket? It may be, but the fact that it is scheduled to take place in the English season and, in 2009 at least, during an England Test series, suggests that it's actually a threat. So give the ICC some teeth and ensure the IPL isn't scheduled at a time when it detracts from other competitions. Including English domestic competitions.

10. Limit the weight of bats

It's a batsman's game. So, by limiting the weight of bats, batsmen will be obliged to time the ball better; cross-batted slog-sweeps will no longer be so prevalent. Let's even things up.

ABSENT, PRESUMED DEAD

Some players won't let anything stop them. Others are more easily put off... SPIN pays a visit to cricket's casualty ward

Derek Pringle

Legend has it that Pringle once injured his back writing a letter and, as a consequence, was forced to miss the Headingley Test against Pakistan in 1982. In truth there is a little more to it: he was actually writing a letter when he leaned back on his chair and it gave way. The fall caused a back spasm. Much less ridiculous.

Pring: letter-writing accident

Don Denton

The next time you hear about a player pulling out of a game because of a hamstring injury, consider Denton, who lost part of his leg in World War I, yet was still selected for Northants upon his return. His war service ensured he was allowed a runner – one of his brothers – by special dispensation. As one opposition captain said: "If any fellow has been to the war and has had his leg off and wants to play, he is good enough for me and can have 20 runners."

Harold Heygate

Cricketers in 1919 clearly weren't in the physical condition they are today. Heygate suffered so badly from gout – the charitable called it rheumatism – that he was unable to make it from the dressing room when Sussex played at Taunton and, when a Somerset fielder appealed, the slow-moving player was dismissed as "timed out." As the scores were level at that time and Heygate was the last man to bat, the result was a tie.

Tony Greig

It's sometimes forgotten what a fine all-rounder Greig was, but his record is all the more remarkable given the disability he had to conquer. Greig was epileptic and suffered several attacks during his career, including on debut in 1971–72 and at Heathrow Airport as England returned from their Ashes trip in 1975. Jonty Rhodes also suffers from epilepsy, while Johnny Briggs once had a fit during a Test in 1899 (after the close of play).

Greigy: overcame epilepsy to be England skip

Arthur Croome

While chasing a ball for Gloucestershire one day, Croome slipped over the boundary and impaled himself on a spike. Had Dr WG Grace not had the presence of mind to staunch the flow of blood with his thumbs, Croome may well have died.

Hall: mugged and shot at

Andrew Hall

They don't come much tougher than the South African all-rounder. Hall was at an ATM in Durban one night in 1998 when a mugger fired six shots at him from close range. Miraculously, four of them missed but one grazed Hall's cheek and another lodged in his left hand. The mugger then took Hall's money and car. To make it worse, Hall was attacked again in 2002 and forced to drive around in his own car for 45 minutes with a gun at his head.

Fred Grace

A fortnight after appearing in the first Test in England (1880), Grace died, aged just 29. It is said he caught a chill staying in a damp bed in a hotel in Basingstoke, resulting in pneumonia.

The Rev Archibald Fargus

While some on this list came back from terrible injury, Fargus actually rose from the dead. Well, sort of. Fargus was reported dead after the ship he should have been on was sunk by a German submarine in World War I. But it turned out that Fargus had arrived late and missed the boat.

5 THINGS RAVI BOPARA TOLD SPIN THIS YEAR

England's No 3 on setting up his own school team, following three ducks with three centuries, and becoming more ignorant…

We were a bit at a disadvantage, coming from an urban area.

A lot of schools don't have cricket. There's not enough facilities, especially in London. There's nowhere to go and play cricket. But then me and the teacher at school worked together to set up a team at my primary school. He did all the organizing and I just tried to get guys involved and come along to the trials. But we organized the team and then we started to win. We won the Lord's Taverners Cup.

I knew my first series would make me better

Sri Lanka 2007 was one of the hardest times of my career. [Ravi hit 42 in five innings and ended with three ducks in a row] It was tough. But I knew, when I got run out in that last game, that I was going to become better from that experience. Because it hurt me so much. Some people are put off by that kind of feeling but I was driven by it. You have to learn from your mistakes.

I got a little too desperate to play for England.

Even before I hit the century for Essex against Australia in 2005, I was getting all that talk about being a future England player. And you can get a little bit desperate yourself and start to believe the hype. That summer, when I was 20, I was thinking too much about wanting to play for England. You start to dwell on negatives a lot. So, with experience, I think I've become a bit more… ignorant. I can blank things out.

I never watched a full day of Test cricket

I watched a lot of cricket on TV when I was growing up – a lot of my hero,

Sachin Tendulkar. I used to watch a lot of one-day cricket live. And a lot of Test highlights. I never watched a whole day's Test cricket, though; just the highlights. What I liked about Test cricket was that beautiful shots that might go for one run in one-day games would go for four in Tests. There was something nice about seeing that ball hop over that rope.

I don't think too much about the bowlers.

I hit centuries in three consecutive Tests, February to May. What changed since my debut series? I try to enjoy myself. I don't think too much about the game or who the bowlers are or what might happen. I never think, "I should score runs today." I just make sure I've prepared as well as I can. If I score runs I score runs and if I don't… then it's not my day.

7 QUESTIONS FOR CHARLOTTE EDWARDS

You bowled New Zealand out for 85 in the ICC World Twenty 20 final. Was winning the title easier than you thought?

I wouldn't say it was easy. I don't think we started playing our best cricket until the semi-final. I guess you have to peak at the right time and we did. But that was a tough semi-final against Australia.

Which felt better, to win the T20 or the 50-over World Cup?

The 50-over was really special, to finally win a world trophy for the first time. Then again, the whole occasion of the Twenty20 final at Lord's – I don't think we'll ever beat that.

How did the team adapt their game for Twenty20?

The girls have tried a lot more things in the nets. I think it will have a big impact on how we play the 50-over game. That run chase against Australia was one of the best we've ever had so that gave us a lot of confidence later in the summer [*the side retained the Ashes and won the ODIs 4-0*].

Your team seems to be one of the best prepared teams in British sport. What do you put that down to?

We've just got the support now, really. The ECB massively back us and everything's just fallen into place. We have a great group of players and great support staff; it's a real professional unit. And we've had the backing from the ECB which has been really a massive part of our success.

Is there still a perception that cricket is not a girls game?

Yeah, I think you're always breaking down barriers, but the awareness is massive now. The profile we've had now after our success means people are more aware of women's cricket and hopefully more and more girls are going to take the game up now. It's about just getting the kids playing and enjoying it. There's so much enthusiasm out there.

Has the Chance to Shine money – that funds eight of the team as part-time professionals, coaching youngsters – made a big difference to women's cricket?

Yeah – it's no coincidence that we've become more professional over the last year and that our success has gone through the roof. So hopefully that will continue and more and more girls will be put on the Chance to Shine contracts. I think they've been vital to our success.

Clare Connor told SPIN that she was looking into putting the women's team into a men's premier league. Do you think that's a good idea?

I'm not sure about playing a full season in a men's league. But we will definitely be playing a lot more warm-up games against men's and academy teams. I think that's the way forward. We did it before this tournament and I think it really helped get the girls out of their comfort zones. We want to keep raising the bar as much as we can. Logistically, I'm not sure there's the time for us to play in a league, but to play more warm-up games against boys would be brilliant.

No Wii for you, young man! The whole year can only be described as a dismal catalogue of frittered opportunity. Yet again, I'm afraid it's a case of "Can do better".

Let's not get too carried away about Christmas. Let's save our energy planning for the big one – Easter.

SECRET SANTAS

Cricketing celebs get into the spirit. But who's behind the beards?

It's Easter, it's definitely Easter! Oh my word, no, it's Christmas! And. Let Me. Tell. You. That. Is. An. Extraordinary. Festival. In. Anyone's Book. I Hev. Never. Seen. A Celebration. Like. It.

It's Christmas, it's yuletide, it's seasonal. You're a young lad, a young man, a Santa fan. I'm a character, a personality, a veteran. I say things three times, three different ways.

I just take every Christmas as it comes and try to get the presents in the right area.

I'm sorry, David. I just don't see the point. I really don't.

Answers: Bob Willis, Andy Flower, Tony Greig, David Lloyd, Monty Panesar, Sir Ian Botham.

SPIN ANNUAL 2010 **29**

THE THIRD UMPIRE'S
CHRISTMAS QUIZ

There's 200 runs up for grabs: getting the lot will, trust us, be impossible.*
*Unless you can access Google and books, obviously. Answers on page 102

OFF THE MARK (46 RUNS)

1. Which Australian state side does Ricky Ponting play for? *(4 runs)*
2. Name the four sides that took part in the 2008 Stanford Super Series [pictured above]. *(1 run each)*
3. England Lions played New Zealand "A" in New Zealand in March; Australia (at Worcester) in July and Australia (at Canterbury) in August. They had a different captain every time. Name the three skippers. *(4 runs each)*
4. Which player has played on the winning side in more Test matches than anyone in history? *(4 runs)*
5. Floyd Reifer took on a high-profile role in July 2009. What was that role? *(6 runs)*
6. Mark Butcher retired this year. He played 71 Tests for England. But – to within five on either side – how many one-day internationals? *(4 runs)*
7. West Indies began their tour of England in 2009 on April 20 in Leicester. Who was their captain? *(6 runs)*
8. Two players captained England this year. Andrew Strauss and... who was the other player? *(1 run)*
9. Which county plays at the St Lawrence ground? *(2 runs)*
10. Who was captain of Yorkshire in 2009? *(3 runs)*

NUMBERS (10 RUNS)

1. Which recently retired England player had played in a total of 651 one-day matches – more than anyone in the history of cricket? *(2 runs)*
2. England's best-ever one-day international bowling figures are 6/31, achieved in 2005 [above] by... whom? *(4 runs)*
3. In 2009, an innings of 303 not out became the earliest-ever triple century scored in an English season. It was hit on April 18 – by whom? *(4 runs)*

ENGLAND v AUSTRALIA (21 RUNS)

1. Name the England XI that won the second final of CB Series in 2007, clinching England's first major one-day series win abroad in over a decade. *(11 runs)*
2. Which bowler was in England's squad for each of the first four Ashes Tests of 2005, but was left out each time, before being dropped altogether for the final Test? *(2 runs)*
3. Only one player from Australia's 1997 Ashes tour party was still in the party for the 2009 series. Who? *(2 runs)*
4. When Graeme Swann and Monty Panesar played together this summer they were the first pair of specialist spinners picked by England in a home Test for 10 years. Who were the England spinners who had been paired in 1999? *(2 runs each)*
5. Which Australian player had a top ten hit in India in 2007? *(2 runs)*

CURIOSITIES (51 RUNS)

1. Who took 12 wickets on his Test debut in November 2008 – but played just one more game before being dropped, apparently for good? *(4 runs)*
2. Who was the last player to open the batting and the bowling in the same Test match? *(6 runs)*
3. Who had already played 23 one-day internationals by the time he made his England debut in May 2009? *(6 runs)*
4. Excluding Mark Ramprakash [pictured], which English batsman, still playing in 2009, has hit the most first-class centuries in his career? *(6 runs)*
5. Which England player was hit for 26 in one over in an ODI by West Indies' Shivnarine Chanderpaul in March? *(4 runs)*

6. What happened in Tests in England in 1939, and in Australia between 1936 and 1979, and hasn't happened anywhere ever since? *(6 runs)*
7. Who was the last spinner to open the bowling for England? *(6 runs)*
8. Monty Panesar was the first Sikh to play for England. Who was the second? *(3 runs)*
9. Which ex-England bowler kept wicket and opened the batting (as well as captaining his side) in a Midlands division Twenty20 Cup match in 2003? *(6 runs)*
10. What noteworthy feat did Brendan Nash achieve by making his Test debut in Dunedin in December 2008? *(4 runs)*

PICTURE ROUND (20 RUNS)

Name these five grounds *(4 runs each)*

TWENTY20 (34 RUNS)

1. Seven English players were with IPL teams during its second edition in 2009. Name them. *(1 run each)*
2. Four counties have never reached Twenty20 finals day, after seven years of the tournament. Name them. *(4 runs each)*
3. Which player has appeared at six Twenty20 finals days out of seven? *(4 runs)*
4. England [above] had a 15-man squad for the ICC World20. They used 14 players – which player stayed on the bench throughout? *(2 runs)*
5. Which player hit 27 from 21 balls on his England debut in March – and was not picked again all year? *(3 runs)*
6. Which 40-year-old was selected in England's provisional squad for the ICC World Twenty? *(2 runs)*
7. Deccan Chargers won the IPL this year: who was their captain? *(2 runs)*
8. Which former England all-rounder's son was the most economical frontline bowler in this year's Twenty20 Cup group stages? *(4 runs)*
9. Which Kent all-rounder has played more games of Twenty20 than any other England-qualified player? *(4 runs)*
10. By August this year only one player had scored an international Twenty20 century. Who? *(2 runs)*

AGES (6 RUNS)

Place the following cricketers and slebs in order of age (youngest first).
1. England opener turned gantryist Nick Knight
2. Dance champ and master batsman Mark Ramprakash
3. Maverick twirler turned pokerist Shane Warne
4. Miniature popstress Kylie Minogue

DON'T FORGET CHECK THE ANSWERS AND YOUR SCORE ON **PAGE 102**

IN COMMON (12 RUNS)

What do the following groups of players have in common? *(4 runs for each correct answer)*

1. Shaun Pollock, Mr Cricket Mike Hussey, Albie Morkel, Shaun Tait, Brad Hodge
2. Brad Hodge, Ed Joyce, Rob Key, Graeme Smith
3. Graeme Smith, Justin Langer, Shane Warne, Kamran Akmal, Shane Watson

HOW GOOD WAS THAT?

Big crowds, close finishes, shock results, new skills: the ICC World Twenty20 was a near-flawless celebration of international cricket. **SPIN** relives a breathless 17 days

DAY 1 (JUNE 5)

After a glorious week of sunshine, the skies darken, the rain falls and the second ICC World Twenty20 begins. At Lord's, England are spared the customary embarrassment of a proper opening ceremony when the stage is deemed unfit for Alesha Dixon (long leg) to take to the field. ICC gaffer David Morgan and the Duke of Kent – seriously – do the honours instead.

The Lord's pavilion is virtually empty.

The customary embarrassment of on-field ineptitude lives on, though, as Paul Collingwood's team come unstuck against a determined, carefree Dutch side. Despite winning warm-up games against Scotland and West Indies with the same team, KP's absence (injured) leads England to field Rob Key, Eoin Morgan and Adil Rashid in what many later suggest to be a complacently experimental team selection. There's no worries as Bopara and Wright put on a century opening stand; no panic even when England muster just 60 from the last nine overs, a pattern that will become familiar. 160 will be enough, surely?

No.

The Dutch play out of their skins, with Tom de Grooth hitting 49 off 30, reverse-sweeping Rashid and hitting Broad down the ground for six. It's a mighty – and a mighty confident – innings and dooms a clearly rattled England. With the rain teeming down, Broad misses three run-out chances and a catch in a tense final over.

Beaten by Holland. A new low.

DAY 2 (JUNE 6)

More rain reduces Scotland's opener After months of listening to no-marks saying that he was wrong to prefer playing Twenty20 for £100k a week in the sunshine rather than Test cricket

Brett Lee, oddly relaxed about Chris Gayle's attempt to end his comeback bid

for 50p a week in the snow, Chris Gayle takes it all out on Australia at the Oval. He began the last World T20 with the first (and still the only) international T20 ton. This campaign starts with an 88 off 55 balls including a six held to be the largest ever seen at the Oval – the highlight of a Brett Lee over that disappears for 27 runs.

Lee's four overs cost 56 as the Windies chase down 169 with 25 balls to spare. It is a thrashing. Afterwards, Punter is philosophical. "If we don't qualify by beating Sri Lanka then we'll have two weeks in Leicester and that's not going to be good for anybody."

India begin their defence of the title with a routine win over Bangladesh at Trent Bridge, with a routine 41 off 18 from Yuvraj Singh turning what threatens to be a mediocre total into one of the highest – 180/5 – of the tournament.

DAY 3 (JUNE 7)

At The Oval, favourites South Africa brush aside Scotland's challenge 211 to 81, but the minnows provide one of the moments of the tournament, as Kyle Coetzer takes a stunning leaping catch on the boundary to remove Mark Boucher.

England, already playing to stay in the tournament, redeem themselves in front of a hyped-up Oval crowd. Man of the match Luke Wright (34 off 16) gets them off to a great start, with Kevin Pietersen's 58 off 38 anchoring the innings' charge to 185/5.

Pakistan are at their Keystone Cops worst in the 48-run defeat. Five

dropped catches. Off-spinners bowling no balls. Fielders haplessly letting balls zip between their legs. Shahid Afridi playing forward defensive shots in the run chase.

DAY 4 (JUNE 8)

More grim weather, with the sight of Sri Lanka sitting on the bench at Trent Bridge, huddled beneath duvets. And yet the tournament continues to spread joy through the land, as the Sirils put the Aussies out.

Gunner Ajantha Mendis (3/20) and Slinger Lasith Malinga (3/36) limit the Aussies to 159/9 off 20. A brilliant, leaping catch on the rope at deep square leg from David Warner removes Jayasuriya to give the Aussies early

Clockwise from left: testing the stage ahead of Alesha Dixon's planned (but later abandoned) opening performance; Netherlands light up the opening night with a shock win over England; Sirils Sangakkara and Mubarak celebrate putting the Aussies out; Punter and Binger ponder the delights of a fortnight in Leicester after their T20 exit.

hope, but the maverick batting of Tillakaratne Dilshan soon puts them on the ropes.

Dilshan's 53 off 32 balls includes four fours in one over from Shane Watson – and the unveiling of his Dentist Shot against the same bowler, pancaking an 85mph ball straight back over his own head, at great risk to his teeth.

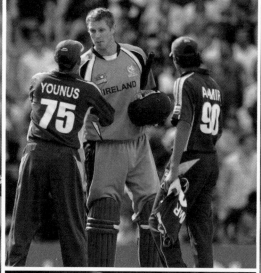

Clockwise from left: KP "comes" "to" "the" "party" with his 50 against the ragged Pakistan; Pakistan put 2007 behind them with a first round win over Ireland; New Zealand get (briefly) on top v South Africa

The Sirils win with an over to spare. The Aussies go to Leicester. Has it really been specifically chosen as the Aussies' bolthole because it has the smallest number of licensed establishments per square mile of any town in the country? (Fact). And Sideshow Symonds has gone home!

Earlier in the day, Ireland virtually secure their place in the Super 8s by springing a shock win over Bangladesh. Kyle McCallan bowls his four overs for 17 before the O'Brien brothers Niall (40 off 25) and Kevin (39 off 17) make mock of the Banglas' four-man spin attack, to chase down their target of 138.

DAY 5 (JUNE 9)

Pakistan do to Holland what the hosts were unable to – give them a sound 85-run trouncing at Lord's. Shahid Afridi takes 4/11. But it is the second match that offers the day's drama. New Zealand are as good with the ball

as South Africa are bad with the bat and the tournament favourites post a paltry total of only 128 runs. New Zealand only lose five wickets in the 20-over chase but it all goes wrong for them as miserly spells from Botha and van der Merwe see the Black Caps fall one run short. South Africa show the world that they are still the world's best fielding unit – and now also, finally, boast a spin-bowling department too.

Virender Sehwag leaves the India squad with his shoulder injury.

DAY 6 (JUNE 10)

Should someone at the ICC have noticed that if points are not carried through to the next stage, you'd get an awful lot of dead rubbers? You'd think so. But today we have two.

The West Indies rest skipper Chris Gayle – he must be exhausted with all that jumping about he has been doing

recently – and put on a below-par show in their defeat to Sri Lanka. Jayasuriya is unlucky not to make a quickfire century, as he is leg-before to Simmons for 81 off 47 balls. Dilshan plays some more extraordinary shots for his 74, also from 47.

The Windies fall 15 runs short. A fine cameo of 51 off 38 from Bravo gives them a sniff, but wickets fall at the right time for the Three Ms – Malinga, Muralitharan and Mendis. The match will be best remembered, though, for a unique piece of fielding from the man no-one (yet) is calling the fourth M: Angelo Mathews. Trying to save a six from Sarwan, he leaps high beyond the rope and, like Ian Bell high-fiving Big Bird Joel Garner, pats the ball back into play. It's a crazy, inspired moment that sends the umpires scurrying for the rule books. The umps side with Mathews – the ball went beyond the rope but didn't land. The MCC later confirms they were right to do so.

Sri Lanka ease past West Indies in the dead rubber in Group C

In possibly the least interesting match of the tournament, Zaheer Khan (4/19) outclasses the Irish batting line-up – he beats Jeremy Bray with all six balls of the second over, with the final delivery sending the hapless Australian-Irishman's stumps flying. India chase the 113-run target with 27 balls to spare.

The absent Sehwag still casts a large shadow over the Indians' campaign: skipper Dhoni refuses to answer questions about his star batter at the post-match press conference and things get heated when a hack apparently accuses Dhoni of leaking allegations about Sehwag to the Indian media.

DAY 7 (JUNE 11)
The first day of the Super 8s. At Trent Bridge, England are outclassed by the ruthless South Africans. Winning the toss, they never recover from losing both Wright and Bopara within the

first two overs. A procession of failed reverse sweeps and elaborate slogs follow, with only Shah's 38 holding things together. Teenage left-arm pacer Wayne Parnell – one of the finds of the tournament – takes 3/14 from his 3.5 overs. The target of 112 is minuscule but South Africa tease/bore us by taking 18.2 overs to get there, with Mr Excitement Jacques Kallis hitting 57 off 49 balls.

Jesse Ryder, slated to be one of the stars of the tournament, departs. "Unfortunately medical advice is that it would be very difficult for Jesse to regain full fitness in time…It's a real disappointment for Jesse. He's one of the most explosive batsmen in the world and was well placed to make his mark on this tournament," says Black Caps team manager Dave Currie, looking at his watch and waiting forlornly outside the Wetherspoons. Of course not. Ryder has a stomach infection and is hospitalized.

DAY 8 (JUNE 12)
A big day at Lord's. First Sri Lanka beat Pakistan by 19 runs. But it's the fact that these two teams, ambushed by terrorists in Lahore in March, are here at all that counts. They line up together for the national anthems, a gesture that puts the tournament in its proper context.

Later, there are momentous events on the park, as West Indies come from behind to defeat the reigning champions India thanks to a magic innings of 66 from 36 balls courtesy of Dwayne Bravo.

Bravo – his all-round T20 game honed by playing with the Mumbai Indians in the IPL – takes four Indian wickets to reduce the champs to 153/7. But well into the last hour West Indies still need 74 runs from 48 balls, with the Indian-dominated crowd sensing another easy win. But then the tension grows and the uproar subsides as Bravo and

Colly is skittled by Jacques Kallis in England's Super8 defeat to South Africa

Lendl Simmons turn ones into twos and pressure the Indian fielders; a straight six off an Ishant Sharma slower ball for Bravo, a reverse-swept four off Harby by Chanderpaul... soon the Indian crowd are headed for the car parks and bus stops; it's down to eight off two overs and Bravo settles it with a six over extra cover off Zaheer Khan.

DAY 9 (JUNE 13)

Umar Gul takes five wickets for six runs against New Zealand at the Oval. The Black Caps think they are struggling at 72/4 from 12 overs. Then Gul comes on mid-innings and skittles them with the best figures in international T20 history.

Gul has help: his first scalp, Scott Styris, falls to a brilliant, running-back-to-the boundary catch from Shahid Afridi. The catch – and Afridi's look-at-me celebration in front of the fans – is possibly the moment of the

tournament. Twice Gul takes two wickets with consecutive balls. The Kiwis are blown away for 99. Pakistan pass them with 41 balls to spare.

Even so, skipper Younus Khan reveals afterwards that he has given up looking cheerful. "People misunderstand my smile," he says, his face now Bob Willis-esque. "They think I am not committed enough playing for my country because I'm always laughing even when we lose. But this is life. You must go forward and leave what has already happened behind you."

Gul's figures are scarcely credible. Here, at the spiritual home of Umpire Darrell Hair, the Black Caps suggest, in fact, they are not credible at all. Vettori asks the umps to look at the ball during the innings and raises the matter with the match referee afterwards. "The amount of reverse swing that we saw was new to us and

therefore we raised a couple of concerns," says Vettori, with an understatement and restraint not wholly matched by the Pakistani fans who immediately leap on to web forums to discuss the matter...

DAY 10 (JUNE 14)

Face down in the last ditch, as ever, England have a tricky away game to negotiate. At Lord's. With the home of cricket three-quarters packed with Indian fans, Colly and co. take badly to being booed during their warm-up; MS Dhoni is allowed to toss the special coin at the start, too, which also gets Colly's back up. As usual, England don't get enough with the bat. Dimi Mascarenhas is moved up to No 4 but ekes out just 25 from 27 balls, with not a sniff of his (erstwhile) trademark sixes. At one stage, England go seven overs with just one boundary – a KP six – a dismal record that they will, as it turns out, have no trouble surpassing.

But India mess things up in a very English way by sending in the rookie Ravi Jadeja at No 4 ahead of Yuvraj and Dhoni. An increasingly panicked Jadeja can't get the ball off the square but also can't get out: he manages just one boundary in 35 balls and by the time Stuart Broad catches him on the ropes, India are sweating over their apparently meagre target of 154.

James Foster's sharp stumping of Yuvraj is a big moment but the tension stays until the very end: even with India needing 15 off three, Yusuf Pathan hits Ryan Sidebottom for a six. But finally, the champions make their exit, flattered by the three-run margin of defeat.

"We were tired when we got here. We weren't an energetic team and never reached the state of intensity required for an international match," says India coach Gary Kirsten afterwards, adding quickly that the seven-week travel and cricketfest of the IPL was In No Way to blame for his side being knackered.

Earlier, Ireland come within 10 runs of chasing down the 145 they need to beat Sri Lanka, after Alex Cusack (3/18) has put the brakes on the Sirils. In truth, it takes a mammoth effort to get that close, with John Mooney biffing 18 off the penultimate over from the world's No 1 ODI bowler, Nuwan Kulasekara.

DAY 11 (JUNE 15)
The day the music dies. Well, the day that England's weird, experimental, stop-start, sporadically hopeful music dies. Bopara (55) and Pietersen (31) again lay foundations for a big score that never materializes, as England manage nine barren, boundary-free overs in the second half of the innings.

Who needs Graham Napier? England?

Even with West Indies missing their injured spearhead Fidel Edwards England are reduced to scampering ones and twos in an underachieving 161/7. Duckworth and Lewis drive

another nail into the coffin with their giant algebraic hammer: after an hour's break for rain, West Indies are set just 80 to win from nine overs. With a soggy but unbowed crowd roaring them on, Ryan Sidebottom bowls Chris Gayle and James Foster pulls off another smart stumping to remove Bravo and leave Windies 45/5. It can't last. Sarwan and Chanderpaul – the most experienced sixth wicket pair in world cricket, surely – see the Windies home.

Afterwards, skipper Collingwood takes the positives – that's the positives of being the country that invented Twenty20 (and indeed cricket) and yet having such low expectations that to reach the last eight of a tournament and not lose every single game is seen as some kind of achievement.

Earlier, Pakistan avenge their 2007 World Cup defeat to Ireland with a 39-run win. That Caribbean calamity is clearly in captain Younus Khan's mind: he says that if Pakistan win the tournament they will dedicate their victory to their late coach Bob Woolmer, who died of a heart attack the night after the Ireland game. Younus also hits back decisively against the Kiwis' allegations of ball tampering: "We're capable and don't need to cheat."

He's not smiling at this point.

DAY 12 (JUNE 16)
The depleted New Zealanders are, crazily, a game away from the semis purely on the strength of victories over Scotland and Ireland. At 93/4, chasing 159 to win against Sri Lanka at Trent Bridge, they are still in it. Then they lose six wickets for 17 runs in four overs and it's finally all over. Ajantha Mendis takes 3/9.

South Africa ease past India in the dead rubber that follows, despite posting only 130 from their 20. Yuvraj, already being booed by certain sections of the Indian crowd for a misfield against England, runs out Dhoni, to put the tin hat on a grim

tournament for the defending champs. Calamitously, they have lost all three of their Super 8 games.

DAY 13 (JUNE 17)
A rest day. But no rest for England's nemeses Mr Duckworth and Mr Lewis. The stattiest men in cricket – and there's some competition – announce they are going to amend their giant abacus. "People have suggested we need to look very carefully and see whether the numbers in our formula are totally appropriate for Twenty20," says Lewis, almost exactly echoing the words of England fans on Monday night. Duckworth adds: "My suspicion is there might be a slight difference but not very much, for instance that West Indian target of 80 might go to 81 or 82."

Oh, stop it.

DAY 14 (JUNE 18)
For the fourth time, South Africa exit a major tournament at the semi-final stage. In a tense back-and-forth struggle with Pakistan at Trent Bridge, they are overcome by a 50 and two wickets from Shahid Afridi as well as the relentless yorkers, again, of Umar Gul. By the time Golden-arm Gul gets on for the 14th over of the run chase, the Saffers need 11 an over. Ingeniously, they have JP Duminy and Jacques Kallis at the wicket, controls set to "Timeless Test". Albie Morkel, controls set to "Frustration", is on the bench. The margin of victory is only seven runs but, in truth, the Saffers are never in it.

DAY 15 (JUNE 19)
At the Oval, West Indies frustrate Sirils veteran Sanath Jayasuriya into changing his bat five (or maybe six) times in his 37-ball innings. At one end, Sri Lanka just can't get going – but at the other, Dilshan is playing one of the innings of the tournament: 96 off 57 balls.

With 158/5, the Sirils don't seem to have enough on the board and Sangakkara's decision to kick off the second half with Angelo Mathews'

Shiv Chanderpaul and Ramnaresh Sarwan celebrate Windies' Super8s victory over England

apparently innocuous medium-pace seems curious. But Mathews picks up three wickets in an incredible first over – all bowled, all dragged on. It's a sensational start and the wickets keep on falling. Soon it's just Gayle versus the strongest attack in world cricket. There seems to be no chance. There isn't. Gayle hits an unbeaten 63 – no-one else makes double figures. Malinga wraps it up with a lethal yorker to remove Sulieman Benn.

DAY 17 (JUNE 21)

Finals day. England's women sweep away New Zealand by six wickets in the first game of the day at Lord's. They become the first English sports team to win a World Cup in anything on home soil since you-know-when.

For the main attraction of the day, Lord's is full of Pakistan fans, with pockets of Sri Lankans thrown in. Still plenty of room to be found in the pavilion, though.

Sri Lanka – the favourites – never recover from losing Dilshan in the first over. Having failed to score off teenage left-armer Mohammad Ameer's first four balls, Dilshan tries an ambitious scoop from the fifth ball, and is caught at square leg. The Sirils are 67/4 by the time Umar Gul comes on for the 12th over; four balls later, they are 67/5. Skipper Sangakkara anchors the ailing innings and bats through from the second over to the last; Angelo Mathews – a great find in all three disciplines – comes in at the end and biffs 35.

The Sirils' maverick bowlers are adept at defending the indefensible. Here, they have to defend 139. Sangakkara uses five bowlers in the first six overs but the Pakistanis – having played the Sirils in March – are not fazed by Mendis and Malinga. Afridi, coming in at No 3, hits 54 off 40. Though the "Afridi, Afridi" chants ring out round Lord's, he does not permit his

supporters to turn his head and limits himself to just four boundaries as he sees Pakistan home by eight wickets.

Afterwards, Younus Khan gives a frankly brilliant press conference that is by turns imperious and hilarious. He makes a plea for other teams to come and play in Pakistan and inspire the local youngsters. He confirms that the win is dedicated to the late Bob Woolmer, who was a "father figure" to the team. As the journalists stand up to leave, Younus calls them back and announces his retirement from international Twenty20. "I'm 34; I'm an old man," he says, in defiance of every official source that has him down at just 31. No-one quite knows why he has suddenly aged.

Younus, draped in a huge Pakistan flag and looking drained despite not having batted, declares the win "a gift for our nation," and allows himself a big – and entirely appropriate – smile.

Shahid Afridi celebrates seeing
Pakistan home in the final at Lord's

TOP RUNSCORERS

T. Dilshan	317 @ 52.83
J. Kallis	238 @ 59.50
C. Gayle	193 @ 48.25
K. Akmal	188 @ 26.85
A. de Villiers	186 @ 37.20

TOP STRIKE-RATE

A.Redmond	177.19
A. de Villiers	155
Y.Singh	154.54
K.Pietersen	152.47
D.Bravo	145.28

(minimum: 100 runs scored)

TOP SIX-HITTERS

Y.Singh	9
C.Gayle	8
K.Akmal	7
D.Bravo	6
A. de Villiers	6

MOST ECONOMICAL BOWLERS

S.Afridi	5.32
N.McCullum	5.42
A.Mendis	5.50
R. van der Merwe	5.62
W.Parnell	5.71

(minimum: 10 overs bowled)

MOST WICKETS

Umar Gul	13 @ 12.15
A. Mendis	12 @ 11.91
S.Ajmal	12 @ 13.58
L.Malinga	12 @ 15.08
S. Afridi	11 @ 13.54

PLAYER OF THE TOURNAMENT

Tillakaratne Dilshan

HOW MUCH IS TOO MUCH?

Fixture congestion has been blamed for Andrew Flintoff's premature retirement from Test cricket. In the 1950s, England played just 83 Test matches; since 2000, they have already played 127 (up to the end of the Ashes), as well as 209 one-day internationals. Yet, largely skipping county cricket, the workload of the modern Test bowler is not necessarily greater: in all forms, Flintoff had bowled the equivalent of 5,315 overs when he announced his Test retirement; Fred Trueman and Harold Larwood managed career totals of 16,781 and 10,492 overs respectively. In 1926, Larwood bowled 971 overs; in 1977 Ian Botham **bowled** 810 overs in all competitions. Steve Harmison has never bowled more than the 600 overs he sent down in all competitions in 1999. And what of Hampshire medium-pacer Derek Shackleton, who sent down 1,000 overs a season 16 times in 17 years (1952-1968) and in 1962 alone, managed 1,717 overs? More recently, even Glenn McGrath "only" managed a career total of 9,641.

SHANE WARNE

Shane Warne's most famous ball – the 1993 Ball of the Century – pre-dated Hawkeye by half a decade, but he continued to bamboozle England's batters right up to his retirement, after Australia's 5-0 Ashes whitewash in 2007. Warne's tally of 708 Test wickets was overtaken by Murali within months but it would take a while longer for English batsmen to forget him.

Here we highlight two occasions where Warne got the better of England. Firstly, at Adelaide in 2006, where England collapsed to a demoralizing defeat on the final day of the second Test. This was the match that turned the series, and it was Warne's performance that made it possible.

Graphic 1 shows the 22nd over in the second innings, bowled to Andrew Strauss. All the balls were similarly paced – the range was between 48.1 to 48.7mph – but the same could not be said for the huge variety of spin and lines employed by Warner. There's no googly – Ball 5 (yellow) is an arm ball going straight on – but Warne created confusion by turning one ball square, then doing something more subtle with the next.

Graphic 2 shows the all-important 34th over, which began with Warne bowling a stunned KP around his legs (red ball), before tormenting

Freddie. Warne did vary his speeds here, between 48.6 and 51.0, and varying his loop and length to try and drag both (big) men forward. With so much variety, Warne was able to dominate all but the greatest batsmen right from the start of an innings.

After mid-career shoulder operations, Warne made little use of the googly – the ball that comes back into the right-hander. But he didn't need to: early in the innings, he would turn a ball several feet, and from that point on batsmen were left to guess exactly when he was going to do that again – or when he was going to bowl a top-spinning flipper, going on straight and coming on to them quicker.

Some batsmen were too clever to be lured by threat of Warne's big turn into playing shots at every ball. Take Andrew Strauss in the 2005 Test at Edgbaston, for example.

Graphic 3 shows the ball that bowled Warne's ball to Strauss, which staggeringly bowled Strauss, middle stump, around his "protective" outstretched front leg from over the wicket. The graphic shows how far outside off stump it would have been (blue line) had it not turned inward (30 inches); instead, it spun almost three feet – also known as a country mile – and egg was left all over Strauss' face.

Play for big turn? Play for no turn? Don't play him at all? Facing Warne was like a game of chess.

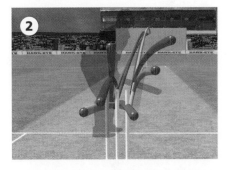

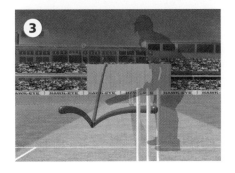

"Well, no-one expects them to hit it there..." Smith and Boucher ponder Plan B

HOW TO SET A FIELD

Our extract from the late Bob Woolmer's coaching bible shows why changes to standard field placements are still so rare...

Fielders have always had the benefit of past generations' trial and error. Today we know where to put the gully when the fast bowler is on, because that's where the gully stood in 1980 and he stood there because that's where the gully stood in 1960 and he was emulating the poor fellow who first had his nose broken by standing too close or had the captain bellow at him for standing too far back.

Fielders stand where they do because that's where the ball goes and has gone ever since overarm bowling reached the speeds recognizable to a modern cricketing audience. As such, field placings in the modern game are more about learning by rote rather than experimenting. That's not to say you shouldn't improvise; but moving

your fine leg very square or moving your mid-off across towards extra-cover just for the sake of experimenting is fairly pointless: the ball will go where it has always gone and as a captain it's your duty to make sure there's a fielder in the way.

The cricket captain must understand the tactical value of each player and how best to use them. It is a waste of skills to put a fast runner with a powerful throwing arm in the slips.

The captain must also know when to set an attacking field – to get wickets – and when to set a defensive one – to save runs – as well as more subtle variations (like an attacking defensive field, for example, where a wicket is captured by frustrating the batsman

and forcing him into a rash shot). You must also be able to communicate your wishes and plans to your team quickly and clearly so that everyone is working towards the same goal.

There are as many potential field placings as there are captains with novel ideas about how best to take wickets. However, these diagrams of basic field settings are gold standards, proven over generations. Use them as starting points and adapt them to your bowling attack, prevailing conditions, the strengths and weaknesses of the batsmen and the state of the pitch.

Extracted from: Bob Woolmer's brilliant 656-page Art and Science of Cricket, *published by New Holland, see page 102 for our special offer price*

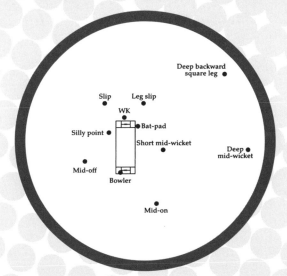

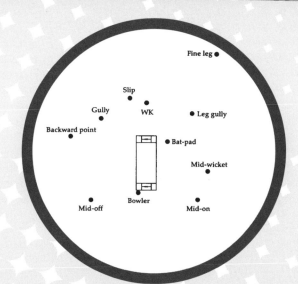

An off-spinner attacking on a good batting wicket

Not a particularly glamorous field, but an important and effective one nonetheless for the spinner turning the ball into the right-hander. Silly point, short mid-wicket and the man under the helmet at short leg apply huge pressure and, if your plan works, the batter may decide to remove one of these close fielders with an aggressive drive straight at him – and nick one or get bowled. Meanwhile, catchers in the deep stay on the alert for slightly more circumspect (but less well hit) chances.

A fast bowler swinging the new ball in or spearing it into the pads and body

Here, your wicket-taking positions are the bat-pad catcher, leg gully and mid-wicket. Mid-on should be standing slightly wider than usual, since the ball will be getting squarer (for a batter able to drill on-drives down the ground, tell your bowler to avoid drive-length deliveries). Don't remove your slip too soon; even if your paceman is peppering middle stump, there's always the chance of a leading edge or even a miscued pull flying to slip.

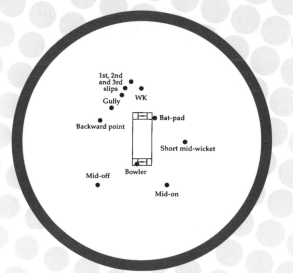

A right-arm fast bowler attacking a right-hander with the new ball

Consider a mid-on if your quick bowler spears the ball into the pads like Makhaya Ntini or is not getting away movement. However, if he is troubling the batter with a line into his pads or body, don't sacrifice your leg-slip by posting him at mid-on; you don't want to see potential singles played into the V only to see a gloved chance or a strangle off the face of the bat fly through a vacant leg-slip area.

An outswing bowler drying up runs while still trying to break through with an older ball

With a softer ball, its varnish hammered off, you're looking to bowl tight lines and keep a lid on scoring, but without sacrificing your wicket-taking options. If your bowler isn't swinging it well and if the batter is settled, the second slip might be a luxury you can't afford but don't go too defensive too soon. The leg gully is also an optional extra, but don't discount the benefit of having a man in there especially if your outswing bowler can start the ball on leg-stump and bend it back towards middle.

Tyron Henderson had already had a good 2008 Twenty20 Cup finals day for Middlesex: in the semi-final, he had blasted 59 off 21 balls to make short work of Steve Harmison and Durham. In the final, a comparatively sedate 43 off 33 had provided good support for Owais Shah's masterful 75. Then, deep into the day's 12th hour of cricket, the finale: with Henderson called on to bowl the final over of the tournament, Kent needed just 12 to win. Lucrative places at the Stanford Super Series and the Champions League were at stake.

It was arguably the biggest over in county cricket history. What was going through your mind?
That's what you practise for. You train for those situations and that's my role in the side: I know that myself and Tim Murtagh will be bowling at the

Kemp drove the last ball back at you too, didn't he? The pressure was still on…
Well, the last ball didn't come back to me too quickly. He stunned it into the ground and took all the pace off it. So it didn't rush me too much. And when I got my hands on it and ran to the stumps to stop the single… I was so happy. There was a lot of relief there. We had a very good evening after that. Some of the boys were still walking round in their spikes at four in the morning in the hotel. It wasn't like you could have a shower when you got back in the changing room.

Every Tom, Dick and Harry was in there with their dog; all the staff – and even Harry Potter was floating around in there. There was champagne everywhere – it was a good evening. Some of the guys were kicked out of

thrown about now and all the new competitions, it's somewhere you want to be and want to get involved with. I do enjoy this format.

You look like the best T20 player in the world. How come you weren't in the first IPL?
I suppose the first season they were going for the high-profile names from all over the world. And they wanted all the hype that goes with that. But Finals Day helped get me in the mix for a contract with Rajasthan Royals for 2009, though.

How close are you to the South Africa team?
[*Sighs*]. Well, I represented my country once [in December 2006]. Fair enough I didn't have a great game. At the time I was playing horrible cricket. I was sitting in the movies when I heard that

TYRON HENDERSON'S NERVELESS OVER

end. That's my job. I always think that if a side needs 12 off the last over and I'm bowling then I back myself not to go for two runs off every ball.

Justin Kemp skinned the first one back past me for four. It happens. He can be a very dangerous man at the end of a game. Then there was the little overthrow on the fourth ball which didn't help. It was messy for a ball or two. Then it all boiled down to the last two balls of the innings. They needed four off two but I managed to prevent that.

The fifth ball was a slower ball…
[*laughs*] Yes. That was a bit gutsy. Very gutsy. Very brave. But Kempy wasn't really expecting me to bowl a slower ball at that stage. I don't think anyone was! It's normally, "Just get the thing in the blockhole". So I took a very high-risk option and sometimes they do pay off.

MIDDLESEX CRUSADERS V KENT SPITFIRES 26:07:08 ROSE BOWL

Tyron Henderson reflects on how he defended 12 runs off the final over to win Middlesex the 2008 Twenty20 Cup

the hotel bar at six in the morning so they could get ready for breakfast.

T20 didn't come along till you were 30. That must have been a Eureka moment for you…
It definitely suits the way I play the game – I just wish it had come through about four or five years earlier, it would have been even better. With all the money that's being

I was called up – that was the Wednesday and the game was on a Friday. So that was hard work, at such short notice. And I was used in a very different role to what I'm used to. [SA coach] Mickey Arthur knew what I could do – he was my coach in the first two seasons of domestic T20 in South Africa and I had very good tournaments: the second one I was player of the series.

Henderson (top left) celebrates T20 success at the Rose Bowl

Now? I can't really be bothered. I've come to England and I want to extend my career over here. I'm not too perturbed about playing for South Africa now, because I don't really think it's on the horizon.

But it's a perfect time to be a Twenty20 specialist, anyway…
That's exactly it. You can play IPL, in England, go back to South Africa. It's almost got to the stage where you can go round the world playing T20 tournaments and not have to play any other forms of cricket. I'm on a one-day contract with Middlesex – if they need me to play four-day cricket, I'm only too happy. My four-day record

isn't too bad. I may have let myself down with the bat but I bat the same in four-day cricket as I do in Twenty20, which can sometimes be to my detriment!

Despite that brutal hitting of Steve Harmison on that T20 finals day, when you started out, you batted at No 10, didn't you?
Like most young bowlers, you only get to bat if you're really needed. And over the years you get a few opportunities with the bat and if it comes off they start to use you a bit more. That's what happened for me. I started off down the order at No 10 and worked my way up to pinch-

hitting roles in one-day cricket. And it seemed to work quite well.

You only debuted in first-class cricket at 24 – was it a struggle to break through?
Yeah – I just floated around a bit after school, went to varsity for a bit and all sorts. I just couldn't get a breakthrough where I was. I was just enjoying life and going nowhere in a hurry. All I wanted to do was play cricket. I'd played at various academies and not really been given the opportunity to take it to the next level. Then I had the chance to go down to the Border cricket academy in East London and Richard Pybus gave me my break in first-class cricket.

SACHIN TENDULKAR

His youth and his time in county cricket, the rise of Twenty20 and his future plus the prospects of India carrying off the World Cup

November 2009 sees the 20th anniversary of the 16-year-old Tendulkar's Test debut. He has now hit more Test (42) and one-day international centuries (43) than anyone, helping to rack up more than 29,000 international runs. That the prodigy's rise coincided with India's increasingly voracious passion for limited-overs cricket has turned him into an international icon.

SPIN caught up with Tendulkar again in London, in June 2009, as he launched his 800-page official autobiography – a mammoth production weighing 66 pounds – via his website, tendulkaropus.com.

As a teenager, you used to play several games a day, didn't you?
My coach wanted me to get as much match practice as possible. So I would just go around town batting in different matches, playing two games a day. I didn't field much – which was a good deal for me! – but I did learn how to build an innings. You learn things you cannot in a net. It helped me develop a match temperament.

When I had done really well in my school matches, I was selected to play first-class cricket for my state. Sunil Gavaskar gave me a pair of pads. It was a huge encouragement for me. I started at a fairly young age. I played

first-class cricket when I was 14. I thought it was fine because I was doing well. I was fearless. I had confidence in my batting; it didn't matter who the bowler was.

Was it correct not to play for India in the Twenty20 form?
I took the decision not to play a couple of years ago and I'm glad. I'm not missing it. It was the right decision.

What did you think about Chris Gayle's comments suggesting that he preferred Twenty20 to Test cricket?
You speak to 10 people and you'll get 10 different opinions. If you ask me, it's got to be Test cricket.

Sachin: 29,000 runs and he *still* gets nervous…

Opposite: celebrating victory in Chennai, 2008

"The mood of the entire nation was low… but at least for a few seconds we were able to put a smile back on faces"

On beating England at Chennai, December 2008

Twenty20 is fun, but Test cricket is far more challenging. So many factors are involved. You have to play well for five days. In T20 you have an hour or 45 minutes to seal a game. There are so many players who have not done well in Test or ODI cricket yet are still successful in T20.

Is Twenty20 cricket pushing the game forward from a technical point of few?
I wouldn't say the game is moving forward from a technical point of view. It's getting more and more innovative, but that's not the same thing. As far as globalizing the game, T20 has made huge progress. The format is ideal if you are trying to enter the non-cricket playing nations. Who knows, maybe 10 per cent of those people introduced to cricket by T20 might find Test cricket interesting.

As a teenager coming to England, was your experience of county cricket beneficial?
My experience of playing county cricket for Yorkshire in 1992 was very useful. Not just as a cricketer but as a person. I think I was the youngest member of the team.. I got to mix with different players and play in different conditions.

I thoroughly enjoyed it. The way they treated me was fantastic. When I went back and played with India I could feel the people of Yorkshire had a soft corner for me. They wanted England to win and me to do well. That's good.

Do you think we are currently in an age of weak bowling?
I don't think the figures support the view that this has been an age of weak bowling. Just look at the spinners: Warne, Murali and Kumble. These three are world-class. And

they've all played in this era. I've played against McGrath, Wasim Akram, Ambrose, Hadlee, Walsh, Botham; all great fast bowlers. There might be some bowler starting now who is seen as great in eight years. There are talented players now. No-one turns into Glenn McGrath overnight. As for the future, Ishant Sharma has developed brilliantly…

Is it true that you originally wanted to be a fast bowler yourself?
I always had a fascination with bowling. I wanted to be a fast bowler, too. I wanted to bat and bowl fast. I did at school level. I opened the bowling. I did everything in that side. Fast bowling, off-spin, leg-spin. It was good fun. I did go to Dennis Lillee's fast bowling camp [MRF Pace Academy, in Chennai] when I was about 12, but he told me to forget bowling and concentrate on my batting. He was probably right.

If we pressed you for one career highlight, what would it be?
The one I'd feel is the best one came in December 2008 when we played England in the Test at Chennai. It was just after the incident [terrorist attacks] in Mumbai. The mood of the entire nation was low. It was a disaster. So many near and dear ones were lost. That cannot be replaced by anything, but at least after we won, at least for a few seconds we were able to put a smile back on faces. That was a big achievement. As one of the members of that Indian team, it means a lot to us. It changed the mood of the entire nation for a while. Something like that was needed.

Do you still get nervous before playing?
I do. I care about cricket and I care about my performances. It's good to

be nervous. It's part of my preparation. Even if I'm playing in an exhibition match, I know I need to be on my toes.

India have become much more successful in recent years. Why is that?
I think the Indian team definitely has more talent today than when I started. We definitely have more match-winners in our team. That was possibly what was missing before. We had match-winners but not as many.

When you start to do well, you play fearless cricket and that's what we're doing today. It's a lot to do with results. In 2000, 2001, we started winning Test matches abroad. Wherever we toured we could beat the opposition in their backyard. That gives you confidence. Gradually that has transformed into a fearless attitude. We have an excellent team. We have very good balance and the ammunition to win the World Cup.

WORLD OF KEMP

Over a period of some years, SPIN class clown ALEX KEMP looked at the world of cricket from the inside, often while bizarrely costumed. He recalls some personal "high" lights…

Training with Kevin Pietersen and Hampshire.

The last time I'd broken into a jog was when I tripped coming out of the all-you-can-eat Chinese buffet some years earlier, so I wasn't expecting too much. But as I did the push ups and star jumps with the Hampshire crew, I started to feel a bit better about myself. Pre-season cricket training didn't seem so hard after all. And when I found I WASN'T in fact the last member of team to finish the sprint round the track I felt for sure a contract at the Rose Bowl was about to be offered. I didn't let the fact that the man I had just beaten over the finishing line was suffering from pneumonia to dissuade me and it was with a sense of crushing

disappointment when I left the training ground with nothing more than a few tips from KP for our readers on how to keep yourself fit.

Cheerleading for Essex Eagles

Further crushing disappointment in my next challenge, but this time for the crowd at an Essex Eagles one-day match when I was roped into performing the cheerleading during the tea interval.

Humiliation abounds as, first, the not inconsiderable Kemp posterior splits the tiny red miniskirt I'd been given to perform the routine in. Then, as I wait for repairs to be made, sitting in the changing room like a condemned man in drag, I was handed a giant Eagles

head and told to make myself useful entertaining the crowd as Eddie the Eagle, the Essex mascot.

My initial scepticism gives way to tentative enjoyment and finally unbridled joy as I walked round the ground in full regalia, getting cheers and waves. Everyone seems happy to see me – a new experience in my column and I give the crowds a dance and pat a few bald men on the head. It all goes wrong though, as I get carried away and start signing my own name when autograph books are thrust at me. Having the costume taken back in disgrace ("they should never think there's a real person in there" I'm told), it's the moment I've been dreading. The skirt has been stitched up, the pom-poms are ready and it's time for me to join the girls out in the middle. The two longest minutes of my life give way to stunned silence as my routine fails to win over a tough Essex crowd and I'm sure, as I

board the train home alone, I hear a long and I think ironic wolf-whistle come from somewhere.

Facing Freddie Flintoff
I once played quite a good standard of cricket. I had played to quite a high level representing Middlesex Schoolboys (I was 26 at the time) but even then I was always inked in the scorebook at No 11. Now, even on a beach, with a fielder in the sea and another in a deckchair, I struggle to get it off the square. So it was with a feeling of dread that I turned up at the Lord's nets.

I was told Freddie wouldn't be holding back and would be bowling his full 90mph deliveries. I was also told to buy a box. I bought three.

Still, I think I dealt with my over of Fred quite well. Yes, the Kemp rear end was dotted with six deep red circles, as if I'd sat in a plate of over-ripe strawberries. Yes, I backed so far to leg as he ran up that I was bulging into the next door's net. And yes my technique was so suspect that Fred wore a permanent expression of comical bemusement. But he didn't get me out. And as he placed a bear-like paw around my shoulders and walked me, chuckling, from the nets, I thought, once again, I just may have improved my chances of that belated England call up.

Getting mentally tough
Perhaps delusion was the problem. My next challenge might have helped. I was to meet Mark Gittos, a sports psychologist who has helped many professional cricketers 'get in the zone'. His practice – involving Neuro-Linguistic Programming – gets the unconscious mind to achieve success and banish negative thoughts. I visited Mark at his home practice and he explained his theories. The way you visualise new information or where you look when recalling an event are all clues as to how your mind works. I ask Mark if it's possible he could bring back Kemp: the Glory Years and he sets to work on what must be his greatest challenge.

He asks me to think of a time when things were going well in my life.

There was a long silence, punctuated only by the sound of the clock ticking in the next room.

He changed tack. "Okay, then: think of a negative experience." Ten minutes later, as I was still reeling off my list, Mark had heard enough. I was politely shown the door: too tough to crack.

12th Man at Surrey
A real privilege this one. I took on the 12th man duties at a competitive Surrey fixture at the Oval – a tour game against Bangladesh A. I pitched up at the Hobbs Gate at 9.30am, telling the attendants to let me through: I'm one of the players. They eyed me, with my carrier bag of socks, old trainers and packed lunch, very suspiciously, but I was soon through and meeting my team-mates.

I used Alec Stewart's old locker where he'd left the message "Remember, it's an honour to wear the brown cap. Always enjoy your cricket and play with honour and fun" (it helped me set off with real purpose and swelling of the chest every time one of the batsmen out in the middle wanted a bit of tape for his glove). After all the hours carrying of drinks up and down the Oval steps, captain Mark Butcher tells me that I could actually get on the field of play as a sub fielder. "When I give you the Sherlock Holmes signal," says Butch, puffing on an imaginary Holmes pipe, "That's when I want you to come on the field."

Sadly the rain falls before any Holmes signal is to be seen and another Kemp dream dies.

Bowling at Charlotte Edwards
I think it's fair to say that my record with the fairer sex has been chequered. And things didn't improve much when I was given the chance to bowl at Ashes winning, World Cup hero, England Women's captain Charlotte Edwards. As I pulled the deerstalker from the mothballs once more and turned up for our net I was already hatching plans. Impress here, a quick visit to the gender re-alignment clinic later and the first class career could be back on track.Sadly things didn't go like that. Everything I offered up was met by a great clanging shot, billowing the sides of the net, and yet another Kemp dream faded away.

WHAT IS A GOOD TEST BOWLING AVERAGE?

Since November 2005, Steve Harmison has averaged 40.05 in 25 Tests. Before that, he was averaging just 27.89. Yet the West Indies' Daren Powell still gets a game and his overall career average is a stonking 47.85 after 37 Tests, only marginally better than Pakistan's Mo Sami whose average of 51.37 after 33 Tests is the worst of any frontline bowler in history with 50 wickets to his name. England's '90s leg-spinner Ian Salisbury's 15 Tests brought him 20 wickets at 76.95 which is right down there – but then Shane Warne's first three series for Australia saw him averaging 49.92. Stats don't tell the whole story. India's lanky teenage pacer Ishant Sharma was acclaimed for having Punter Ponting's number on the 2008 tour of Oz – yet finished the series averaging 59.66. Oddly, the worst Test bowling average of all-time is "only" 129.00 – the record belonging to Sri Lankan umpire Asoka de Silva, who took eight wickets in his ten Tests, conceding over 1,000 runs in the process. Then again, Bryce McGain (0/149 off 18) doesn't have, and may never get, an average at all…

GLENN McGRATH

Glenn McGrath was one half of the mightiest double act in Test history, pairing up with Shane Warne to share an almighty 1,945 international wickets. McGrath was a byword for accuracy: if you had five pounds for every time lazy journalists described his bowling as "metronomic" you'd have, roughly speaking, quite a lot of money. His succcess was based on sheer consisteccy and accuracy, allied to the fact that, at 6ft 5, he could get plenty of bounce without needing to dig the ball in all that short.

Here, we focus on two key match-winning performances from McGrath, one from the 2005 Ashes, the second from the 2007 World Cup.

Day 1 of the 2005 Ashes and all is going well for England, with the Aussies bowled out for 190 before tea. Then – disaster. Normal service is resumed. McGrath, bowling from the Pavilion End, removes Marcus Trescothick, Andrew Strauss, Michael Vaughan, Ian Bell and Andrew Flintoff – five wickets in six overs – to leave England 21/5.

Graphics 1 and 2 show his bowling to left-handers (Trescothick, Strauss) and right-handers (Vaughan, Bell, Flintoff) in this spell, with black balls denoting wickets. His three right-handed victims were all bowled. Bowling from very close to the stumps, McGrath bowled most of his balls in a tight cluster; to the left-handers, he pitched the balls on the stumps, angling them towards their off-stump.

To right-handers, they went unerringly outside off-stump. Only once in the entire innings at Lord's did he pitch one up or drop short.

Even when he didn't get wickets, McGrath's accuracy generally kept the lid on batsmen. He missed the second Test of that series, England hit 390 on the first day and… does anyone remember what happened next?

Graphics 3 and 4 show McGrath's 3/18 off eight overs in the 2007 World Cup semi-final against South Africa, when he took three early wickets and ended with figures of 8-1-18-3.

Graphic 3 shows a typical McGrath over, with AB de Villiers playing out the match's fourth over for a maiden. It shows McGrath's ability to land the ball just back of a natural good length and move it slightly either way. It was this ability to make it either seam in or out that continued to draw batsmen into playing shots.

Graphic 4 is McGrath's pitchmap to right-handers in that innings. Just seven balls are pitched outside the main grouping. (Red represents dot balls.) The white balls are his two wickets of right-handers: seeing Kallis advance to meet him in the sixth over, McGrath fired in a yorker to clean-bowl him.

His dismissal of Boucher came from a standard McGrath delivery, holding its own outside off-stump and inducing an edge to Matty Hayden at slip.

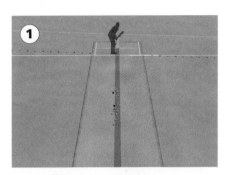

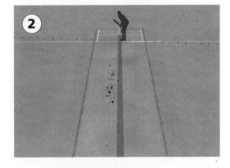

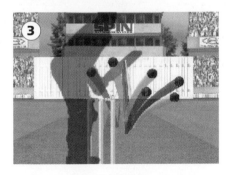

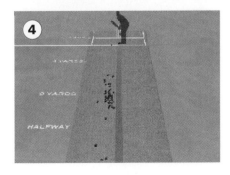

1928–29

A 4-1 series victory in Australia gives Walter Hammond's men the No 1 position, with a healthy margin of 34 ratings points over second-placed Australia. Four teams were now ranked, after West Indies were added to the ranks of Test-playing nations.

1954–55

England didn't lose a series for eight years between 1950 and 1958 – they regain the Ashes in 1953 and, in retaining them with a 3-1 series victory over Australia in 1954/55, go back to the top of the table, where they stay until 1958–59 –their longest stay at the top. The 1956 England team **(left)**, with 122, achieved their highest ratings total since 1890, and did so with a 2-1 series victory over Australia. England's star men were spinner Jim Laker **(below)** who took more wickets than anyone in the 1950s (162 at 18 each) and Peter May who hit 13 centuries and averaged 49.20.

1958–59

After three successful Ashes series, England came unstuck – they lost 4-0 to Australia and also lost the top spot.

1968

England, led by Colin Cowdrey **(below)**, took over the No 1 spot after their 1-1 draw at home to Australia in 1968. But the table is tight, with just a handful of rankings points separating the top four teams. In 1969-70, South Africa thrashed Australia 4-0 to put them miles ahead as the world's best team. England's 2-0 win Down Under in 1970/71, under Ray Illingworth, means that South Africa's 1970 tour of England would have been a play-off for the world No 1 spot: but the Saffers' exclusion from world cricket due to the apartheid boycott meant that England inherited the top spot by default. England's 1971 team's rating (122) was, with the 1956 team, their joint highest of the 20th century.

HITTING THE HEIGHTS

A look at the statistics reveals that England have only been the world's No 1 Test team four times in the last 100 years

1909/10

The only time that England have actually been ranked as the worst team in the world. At this point there were only two other Test teams: England lost series 4-1 in South Africa (1906) and Australia (1907) as well as losing the 1909 Ashes at home.

How we did it

While the ICC's official Test rankings are a recent invention, we have applied the table's rules to all Test history.

This gives a "rating" to every team after every Test, so we can plot not just England's ups and downs in the historical rankings but also compare the strength of every Test team ever. (Ricky Ponting's Aussie team of 2007-08 comes top, with a rating of 143.) Our graph shows the world ranking of the England team over time, peaking in the mid-'50s and plummeting in the 1980s.

Highest-rated England teams since 1900

1. Peter May's team that won a third successive Ashes series in 1956: 122
2. Ray Illingworth's team that won the Ashes 2-0 in Australia (1971): 122
3. Percy Chapman's team that won the Ashes 4-1 in Australia (1928/29): 121
4. Mike Brearley's team that won 5-1 in Australia (1978/79): 119
5. Michael Vaughan's team that won the 2005 Ashes: 119

1974/75

The triumph is short-lived: having lost home series to India (1971) and West Indies (1973) for the first time and then been blitzed 4-1 by Lillee and Thomson's Australians in the 1974/75 Ashes, England slump to fifth place (out of six teams) in the table.

1987–1990

Although Mike Gatting **(below, right)** led England to win the Ashes from Australia led by Allan Border **(below, left)** in 1986/87, England spent the following three years in sixth place out of seven in the rankings. By 1990, the rating is just 79 points – their worst since 1909/10.

2005

England's 2-1 Ashes victory under Duncan Fletcher and Michael Vaughan **(above)** sees them climb to No 2 – their highest position since 1982/83. However, the success is short-lived: after defeat to Pakistan in December, England slip from second to third before the end of the year.

1978/79

With West Indies knocked off the top following a 1-0 defeat by India, England regain supremacy, following a 5-1 crushing of an Australian side weakened by World Series Cricket defections. The result and the rating flatter England. The West Indies soon resume top spot (and hold it for the whole of the '80s), as England's era of Botham **(above)**, Gower and Gatting produces some glorious wins over Australia and some dreadful defeats against pretty much everyone else. The Ashes win of 1986/86 is, in truth, a play-off for fifth position in the rankings against one of the statistically worst Australian teams in Test history.

1999

Another decade, another low-point: England play 13 series away from home in the '90s – and manage just two series wins, both against New Zealand. Home defeats to Pakistan ('92 & '96) and Sri Lanka ('98) signal a slide – while the defeat to New Zealand at home in 1999 confirms them as "the worst team in the world" in Nasser Hussain's first series as captain (and the last series before Duncan Fletcher took over). In fact, England are still rated higher than Zimbabwe. But even so.

2008–2009

Home defeats to India (2007) and South Africa (2008), coupled with away defeats in Sri Lanka (2007/08) and India and West Indies (2008/09) take England down to sixth… even the famous Ashes win of 2009 under Andrew Strauss **(right)** raises them (so far) only to the fifth slot…

DARREN GOUGH

After 20 seasons and 855 first-class wickets, Darren Gough retired in 2008. He reflects on the art of reverse-swing, the delights of getting free golf clubs and the virtues of having a bit of ticker

FIRST first-class wicket

It was in my first game, against Lord's at Middlesex in April 1989, and it was Paul Downton, caught by Arnie Sidebottom at slip. I were only 18, and I got five wickets in the match, including Mike Gatting.

LAST first-class wicket

Justin Langer, caught behind in my last game against Somerset at Scarborough in September 2008. It was set up for it to be an Aussie really. It was funny because, from my last two balls, Alfonso Thomas backed away and gave me a real chance: we had all the fielders up and he slogged them both for four. I took my hat off to him but I was pretty glad to be honest because I wanted my last wicket to be Langer.

FIRST Test win

It was against South Africa at the Oval in 1994. It was great. I got a few runs and Devon Malcolm got nine wickets in the second innings or first innings – I can't remember which. I got the one, though: Darryl Cullinan, caught slip. So I got the best player out. I think he was on 94.

I had added 70 in about an hour with Phil DeFreitas the night before, which turned the match. It was getting dark and we were in the poo. I always liked batting alongside someone who was aggressive, like Pete Hartley at Yorkshire or Daffy with England, because it became a competition. That night we just decided to tee off and take it to them. It was just unbelievable: Daffy tucked into Allan Donald for the last few overs. But I think I started it, and then Daffy just got better and better as the evening went on.

LAST Test win

That was at Headingley in 2001. We were outplayed really, and it was only because of Australia's arrogance, and the fact they wanted to win the series 5-0, that we won. Gilchrist, who was standing in as captain, set us a target and we absolutely walked it. Mark Butcher [173 not out] was magnificent: they couldn't bowl at him. Everything they threw at him he'd either cut it or drive them through the covers for four. It was just amazing to beat them; it didn't matter that the series was gone. They didn't give us an easy total – it was over 300 – but we just played really well.

FIRST time that I bowled reverse-swing

I remember taking 8/0 when I was 15, and I was swinging it then, but it was normal swing. I first started to reverse it in 1993: that was a big year for it, using Reader balls, and I reversed it a long, long way. I taught myself. Watching Pakistan in 1992 was probably the turning point. I just saw Wasim and Waqar and thought, "If

FIRST Test

New Zealand at Old Trafford in 1994. Actually the thing I remember is getting a free set of golf clubs. We got glasses, shoes and golf clubs, and as a young lad that was amazing. I thought: "This isn't a bad job". I remember getting a half-century – I was batting with Daffy again, which

was always good fun – and then got Mark Greatbatch caught at slip in my first over. It was a great Test: we would've won it but for Martin Crowe getting a century.

LAST Test match

South Africa at Lord's in 2003. I knew probably before starting the game that it was going to be my last Test. When I look back now I probably retired too early from Test cricket, but my knee was a mess at the time. I'd had so much surgery and not really been given the right rehab, and I was in that much pain playing I was just glad to get it over with.

FIRST England tour

Australia, 1994/95. I'll never forget getting off the plane and walking through customs at Perth Airport, and I've never seen so many cameras in my life. Absolutely amazing. And that just made me think, "Right, I'll have this: this is what I'm made of; this is my opportunity". I always did well against Australia in Australia. Goochie and a

"I always did well against Australia in Australia. Goochie called me Box Office"

I can do that at that pace it'll be very effective". And it was.

few other people always called me Box Office: the bigger the game the better I performed. That's just something that's within you.

A lot of bowlers have gone over there and struggled. You have to be willing to go at them, as they come at you, and believe. There's times when I've had 0/100 and ended up with three or four wickets for 120. You just never give in.

I remember my first Ashes wicket, which was David Boon at Brisbane. It nipped back, he left it and was bowled. He was always someone I wanted to get out. I tended to pick one player from each team; in that first Test it was David Boon and I got him out with a beauty and that gave me so much pleasure.

LAST England tour
I went on the Ashes tour in 2002/03, but the last tour I played a Test on was in Sri Lanka in 2001 [Gough took 14 wickets @ 19.57 as England won 2-1]. What's the secret to doing well on the subcontinent? Heart and variety – that's all you need. People forget that I was Man of the Series in three of my last four full series for England. I were flying, and then I got my knee injury. Who knows what could've happened?

It was a big loss for England and for me. I could've got a hell of a lot more than 220 Test wickets.

FIRST time I met KP
It was in a club in London, after an England game. He was in there with his girlfriend at the time, and everybody was saying, "Ah that's him, he's South African, he's scoring loads of runs". A lot of negative things, basically. Then I met him when we were in South Africa in 2004/05: Duncan Fletcher told me that there was a lot of things being said about him that were not good.

So Duncan says "Can you look after him?" I said, "'Course I will". Within five minutes, I thought, "What's all the fuss about?" He was a great guy. We're just so much alike in our cricket

thinking and the way we play the game and the way we like to be off the field: very dedicated cricketers who enjoy their downtime.

I wasn't surprised he became captain in 2008. He's got tremendous spirit and a great cricket brain. When we had team meetings he was always the one who came up with a theory for a certain player.

FIRST TV show appearance
God, there's been so many… I think it was *Surprise, Surprise* with Cilla Black. Some lady who really wanted to meet me…

LAST TV show appearance
Hole In The Wall. It was alright except for the outfit. That wasn't very flattering but, yeah, I enjoyed it.

CELEBRATION TIME!

Shake hands calmly and carry on as if nothing's happened? Jump up and down and wave your underpants in the air? **SPIN** lines up some classic celebrations and adds idle, semi-funny captions. Hurrah!

1. Corky Cork, a Lord's hero in 2000. A special message for his girl. "I've had three successful comebacks to the team," possibly.

2. Nass at Lord's, 2002. "Just three more years to wait, fellas, before a complete turnaround in my views on the value of the cricket media."

3. Pigeon McGrath: he invented that thing where the bowlers hold up the ball after a five-fer, of course.

4. Too cool for school Chris Gayle: he's over the moon! You should see him when he's depressed!

5. Yousuf Youhana! He's a Christian! He celebrates every ton by crossing himself and looking to Heaven!

6. Mohammad Yousuf! He's a Muslim! He celebrates every ton by getting on his knees and facing Mecca!

7. Robbie Fowler got a four-game ban and a £32,000 fine for this! Will these people never learn?! All Makhaya Ntini sniffs is success after a Lord's five-fer in 2003.

8. Jonah Jones shows Hayden to the pavilion at Edgbaston last year with a gesture that earned a sizable fine.

9. Greenfingered Brett Lee starts up his lawnmower. Go on, let yourself go son. But if you thought THAT was irritating...

10. NOW, he's moved on to the cheerleader leap! "Oh, Punter, you're so fine." Etc etc

11. Binger celebrates a "wicket". Aleem Dar's hand of doom sticks out to signal the futility. Difficult not to laugh, isn't it?

12. Well, the England one-day side has had its knockers. Fred's fancy dress stag night gets out of hand.

BANNED

As the bans on the "rebel" T20ists are lifted, we survey cricket's history of sending miscreants to Coventry – and, often, inviting them back again

Salim Malik and Hansie Cronje, 2000
Found guilty of match-fixing and banned from cricket, along with Ajay Sharma, Ata-ur-Rehman... and ex-India captain Mohammad Azharuddin – though Azhar's ban was lifted in 2006.

Windies rebels, 1983
The 18 Windies players who went to South Africa, including Lawrence Rowe, Sylvester Clarke and Colin Croft, were given life bans from international cricket – but they were lifted in 1989.

Ed Giddins, 2004
Banned for betting £7000 against his own Surrey side in a Sunday League game in 2002. (He had retired anyway, in 2003.) Previously banned for 18 months, in 1996, for using cocaine.

Graham Gooch, Geoff Boycott, 1982
The 15 English cricketers who went on the rebel South Africa tour in 1982 were paid a reported £40,000 for the three-week trip – but were barred from international cricket until 1985, when Gooch returned for the Ashes.

Mike Gatting, David Graveney, 1989
The pair led the ill-fated 16-man rebel tour party to South Africa. However, they got back up off the canvas (along with fellow tourist Matthew Maynard) to take up high-profile posts with ECB in later years.

Shane Warne, 2003
Tested positive for a banned diuretic, which he said he had taken to slim down and look good on TV. His mum had given him the pill. "I feel that I am a victim of anti-doping hysteria," moped Warner.

Shabbir Ahmed, 2005
Pakistan bowler banned for illegal action. Chucking suspects in previous eras were simply no-balled out of the game permanently.

Herschelle Gibbs, 2000
Banned for "conspiring in match-fixing": he agreed to take $15,000 via skipper Hansie Cronje to score less than 20 in an ODI. (He actually scored 74.)

Shoaib Akhtar, 2007
Received ban and a fine of US$57,000 after hitting team-mate Mo Asif in dressing-room bust-up in the build-up to the ICC World T20.

WILL A WOMAN EVER PLAY FOR THE ENGLAND MEN'S TEAM?

England's women won the World Cup last year. But could a leading female player ever make a career in the men's game?

Clare Connor ECB head of women's cricket

I'm a believer that girls with potential and high skill level and the self-confidence should play with boys as teenagers. Charlotte Edwards [pictured] has done that, Claire Taylor has done that. I did it. I want to facilitate more girls playing in good cricket schools, where they've got to prove themselves even more than if they were playing in an all-female environment. Of the girls in England's World Cup winning squad and the England academy I think about 80 per cent have played competitive boys' and men's cricket.

The next stage of the debate is if you then keep those girls in a male environment, how good can they be? Sarah Taylor and Holly Colvin were both on the Sussex academy for three years. If there wasn't such a thing as women's cricket and they had stayed and maybe got a chance to play second XI men's cricket and their skills level had to adjust and pace and power… we don't know. Their pathway is to play for England women.

Can we start looking at how we identify potential players; can we look at girls who are playing netball, hockey, tennis?

I think a breakthrough can happen. I would have thought it would be a spinner or a batter or a keeper. Claire Taylor is in her early 30s and in great physical condition: on a (physical)

level, she'd be up to the standard of 30 per cent of male first-class players. She's our most mature athlete.

When I had my job interview with the ECB in 2007, I said I'd like to investigate putting our best players either into men's premier league teams on a Saturday, or entering them as a team, so that they're in a hard environment every week. That's still something I haven't ruled out.

The system as it stands isn't designed for women playing first-class cricket, because the counties have to produce cricketers for the England (men's) team. But if we want to develop, say, fantastic wrist spinners it might be that women have got more supple wrists. Maybe for women cricketers to kick on we do need to be playing more men's cricket at a higher level.

Paul Barratt EIS Biomechanist

More scientific training methods mean men and women are in better condition, but the gap in their potential strength and power will always be there. Men's joints are stiffer and stronger so they're able to resist forces that would cause injuries to a woman. Length and proportion of levers are important: men are generally taller and rangier. Wider hips, as women tend to have, can cause you more issues from an injury perspective, because that can impact the way you run and the way is force is distributed around the joints.

Craig Ranson UK Athletics chief physiotherapist, formerly ECB lead physiotherapist

There are female athletes who are powerful enough but they go into other sports rather than cricket. At Loughborough in 2008/09, we had six of England's best young (male) fast bowlers – people like Maurice Chambers and Chris Woakes – doing some lifting in the power weights gym. They were next to some of the female high jumpers of the same age and around the same sort of build and the boys were squatting around 150 kilos and the girls were squatting 160, 180 kilos.

Watching Clare Taylor and Charlotte Edwards (England batsmen) bat against fast young male bowlers in the nets, they have no problem coping with the speed. And, power-wise, you don't have to be hitting sixes in Test cricket: just look at Alastair Cook.

Twenty20 cricket and 50-over cricket are probably further away from women competing, because of the importance of speed around the ground and being able to throw the ball hard and flat. But as a Test cricketer where it is potentially more skills-based, there is no reason why a female player could not compete.

In athletics, which is about pure power, women's performance is not as good as men's. But given the context of cricket, which is more skills-based there are certainly enough women athletes who are powerful enough to perform at cricket.

Ian Crump England women's conditioning coach

All things being equal, women will never be able to compete with men physically. But there is a massive discrepancy within both the men's and women's squads. The top-conditioned men are much better than the women, but there are others whose level of conditioning isn't great. The top women in the England squad would be pushing them.

Spin I would say is the most likely. There is less power involved than fast bowling. I don't know of any woman who can bowl at 90mph, though if you could teach [UK javelin champ] Goldie Sayers to bowl she could potentially get close.

Being able to hit a ball is about timing not power; in any case, our top-conditioned women have enough power to hit fours and sixes. At first there was a problem with injuries and we had to get them more robust. Now, we're making them athletes. The men are trying to do it too, but they tour so much their opportunities for strength work are limited.

IN BRIEF

- Catherine Fitzpatrick, regarded as the fastest-ever woman bowler, was recorded at 75mph
- "We cannot compare women's cricket to the men's game," says India's Anjum Chopra, who has played in the last four World Cups. "Pure strength is the basic difference – we just can't hit sixes out of the stadium and, in terms of entertainment, that really sets us apart"
- Women play at the top level of English (men's) club cricket, so is the divide at higher levels cultural as much as physical? Are the world's best female athletes really not as fast and powerful as the least fit male international cricketers?

HOW CRICKET BECAME A BATTER'S GAME

70 all out used to be a great score. Now anything less than 400 is below-par, and some of the reasons can be surprising

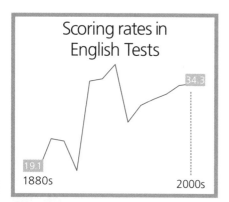

Scoring rates in English Tests

19.1 — 1880s
34.3 — 2000s

1811

Umpires made responsible for choosing the pitch.
Favoured: Batsman.
Why: The choice had originally been up to the visiting side, anywhere "within 30 yards of the centre fixed by the adversaries". The leading bowler of the opposition could pick an area he thought he could best exploit.

1811

No-balls could now be scored off.
Favoured: Batsman.
Why: Previously a no-ball was declared dead. Now the batsman had more scoring opportunities – and a free hit to boot.

1823

Height of wicket raised from 24in to 27in and width from 7in to 8in.
Favoured: Bowler.
Why: More to aim at. Of course.

1829

No-balls not scored off incurred a one-run penalty.
Favoured: Batsman.
Why: Upped the scoring.

1830

Edwin Budding, of Gloucestershire, signed an agreement for the manufacture of his new invention – the lawn mower.
Favoured: Batsman.
Why: The technology now existed to improve pitches. The mower didn't pass into widespread use overnight, though; rabbits, sheep and scythes, remained prime grass-cutters for a while longer.

1835

Round-arm bowling legalized.
Favoured: Bowler.
Why: Originally, bowlers had bowled the ball along the ground. Then came the practice of pitching the ball underarm. During the 50 years to 1770, the average score per wicket had been 7.5; by 1810 it had risen to 13. In the 1820s, bowlers began to strive for greater pace by bowling with a higher action: by 1830, runs per wicket had fallen to 10. By 1840, when the new style had been formally adopted, it was down to nine.

1849

Laws changed: it is now perfectly acceptable to sweep and roll pitches before each innings.
Favoured: Batsman.
Why: Worm casts, which would make the ball's pitch unpredictable, could now be removed.

1864

Over-arm bowling made legal.
Favoured: Bowler.
Why: Accurate bowling became a lot easier.

1870

Heavy roller introduced to the game, at Lord's.
Favoured: Batsman.
Why: It brought an immediate improvement in pitches. WG Grace became the first man to score 2,000 runs in a season, and runs per wicket now stood at 17.

1871

WG Grace scores 2,739 runs in the season.
Favoured: Batsman.
Why: WG raised expectations as to what batsmen could achieve. That year he averaged 79 – the next best average was 34. By then, the 25-year-old had scored more than 10,000 career runs – more than any man. His career average stood at 61; the next best was Richard Daft's 29.

1880s

Rubber grips for handles introduced.
Favoured: Batsman.
Why: For a better grip. Naturally. And they acted as a shock absorber.

1884

Boundary lines introduced "where necessary".
Favoured: Batsman.
Why: Previously, all scores had to be run in full. However, in practice, boundaries had existed on many grounds since the 1860s, for the benefit of showing where crowds could safely watch.

1887

Contact lens invented.
Favoured: Batsman.

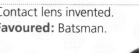

Why: A moving ball is harder to see than a stationary wicket!

1910

Law change: six runs now awarded for any hit that doesn't touch the ground before going over the boundary rope.

Favoured: Batsman
Why: Previously, sixes were awarded only for hits out of the ground. When Gilbert Jessop made two centuries in a match against Yorkshire at Bradford in 1900, he hit eight sixes out of the ground, and almost as many blows again cleared the ropes on the full but earned him only four.

1927

Ball circumference reduced from 9– 9 1/4in to 8 13/16–9in.
Favoured: Batsman.
Why: The 1920s and 1930s were a batting paradise, with pitch preparation having been much improved and the design of the ball with its small seam offering little help to the bowlers. So a smaller ball was introduced. However, the new ball proved harder to catch and many bowlers also found it harder to swing.

1931

Wicket increased in size to 9in by 28in.
Favoured: Bowler.
Why: Larger target.

1937

New lbw rule.
Favoured: Bowler.
Why: An experiment of 1935, whereby the batsman could now be given out even if the ball had pitched outside off stump, so long as he was hit in line with the stumps, was now made law.

1963

First 18-county, limited-overs tournament.
Favoured: Batsman.
Why: Batsmen grew to learn new ways of scoring. The rate of scoring acceleration has increased consistently. In ODIs in England in the 1970s it was 3.77 runs/over; in the '80s, 4.15; in the '90s, 4.59 and 4.82 so far this decade.

1969

Front foot rule introduced for no-balls.
Favoured: Batsman.
Why: Bowlers who dragged their back foot had been able to bowl the ball from in front of the popping crease, that is, from 18-20 yards, under the old rule.

1978

Australia's Graham Yallop becomes first man to bat in Test in a helmet.
Favoured: Batsman.
Why: Protective clothing has taken away some of the fear – and need for good technique against the short ball.

1999

Steve Waugh becomes Australian captain; Adam Gilchrist's Test debut.
Favoured: Batsman.
Why: Waugh began a policy of intimidatory batting, asking his side to score at four an over. Other sides adapted to keep up. Key to this policy was Gilchrist, an ODI regular who made 81 off 88 balls on his Test debut.

2003

Twenty20 launched.
Favoured: Batsman.
Why: To pressurize the opposition.

BobWillis'

GREATEST HITS

SPIN TV reviewer The Third Umpire salutes Sky Sports' nay-saying Pope of Mope

April 17 2007:
England exit the World Cup

England's do-or-die game with South Africa comes to an end a full 30 overs early. An enraged Willis opens his thesaurus at the "Rubbish" page…

1 minute England's batting is "totally STATIC AND STAGNANT… It's the same old story. Apart from Kevin Pietersen and Paul Collingwood, it's been EMBARRASSING."

3 mins Use of "NONSENSICALLY" vis-a-vis England and Powerplays.

6 mins Voice cracks with bafflement and rage: "Come the last ten overs, there's Bopara or Nixon with the RATS AND MICE down the bottom of the order. It's ABSOLUTELY HOPELESS!"

8 mins "Flintoff has been batting like a BLIND MAN, unfortunately."

12 mins "The English public aren't going to put up with it anymore. HEADS WILL ROLL! And those heads should be Graveney, Fletcher and Vaughan. They've all GOT TO GO!"

24 mins "The fall guys are likely to be Graveney, Fletcher and Vaughan from this DEBACLE but the real GUILTY PARTIES are the county chairmen and the members they represent."

29 mins "Have a look at the record of England's under-19 team," suggests Bob. "It is absolutely appalling."

36 mins "When we played," says Willis to host David Gower, "We didn't HAVE a coach." He says this as if having a team coach was as far-fetched as having a team pantomime horse.

37 mins A job description of sorts for the new coach. Of sorts. "Part of his brief is to go round and visit these DINOSAURS in the county committee rooms." His voice again cracking with rage, he adds: "They've had it their way for the last ONE HUNDRED YEARS PLUS! It hasn't worked!"

BATTING LIKE A BLIND MAN

42 mins Willis wants an MD for the England team. "I'm not doing Phil Neale down," says Bob, as he prepares to do the England manager down. "But he's basically just a BAG CARRIER: he puts LABELS ON THE LUGGAGE and organizes taxis and PAYS THE HOTEL BILLS."

45 mins Willis has a view on players who don't like foreign travel. People like Trescothick and Harmison. Is it sympathetic? Er, no. "I'm afraid if you can't do that," says Willis. "You're in the wrong job, mate."

51 mins Willis builds to his finale: "You can't have old SEADOGS trying to stretch out their career into the next World Cup. We must plan with a YOUTH CULTURE rather than a DRINKING CULTURE."

"Well," says Gower, visibly drained, "Some complicated issues there. Debated at some length."

And goes to a break.

February 7 2009: England 51 all out in West Indies

England's third lowest all-out score in Test history? "What's the effect going to be on Andrew Strauss?!" sneers Willis gleefully. "It must be the shortest honeymoon period in history for any England captain!" Soon he's in full flow: "There's a lot of work still to be done. I think it needs to be done in the head. They're MENTALLY WEAK."

"There are more backroom staff than players now! It's absurd! The players don't need all this pampering and molly-coddling. When you're out in the searchlight in the middle... it's down to you, mate. Batting coaches! Bowling coaches! Fielding coaches!" intones Willis, incredulous.

"I'm not going to pussyfoot around," he promises, thrillingly. "I want to make a clear statement here. I'm putting the Dumbslog Millionaire up to No 3; Bell carrying the drinks... and as for Steve Harmison," he concludes, magnificently. "I'm afraid it's back to the dartboard in the Ashington Working Men's Club."

February 2008: England lose by 189 runs to New Zealand

"What," demands a glum-looking Willis re: Steve Harmison, ahead of Day 2 "is his place in the side? Is he the strike bowler, bowling at 90mph, hitting people on the head? Or is he a medium-paced dobber who does a job as a stock bowler. It would appear the latter's the case. "And that," concludes Bob, sounding just like the Reverend Ian Paisley, "SIMPLY CANNOT BE RIGHT."

"This is his profession! He's highly paid! For some reason, they've let him retire from one-day cricket!" he rants, implying that somehow the management might be able to physically force players to take the field. How? Tethers? Blinkers?

Willis keeps his eye on Harmy throughout the Test. He greets his opening spell on Day 2 thus: "Little more than military medium. Really negative body language emanating from Harmison." Then Harmy is dismissed second ball on Day 4: "Harmison's problems continue!" roars Bob triumphantly. "He's got a golden duck to add to his lacklustre bowling performance!"

August 23 2009: England win the Ashes

The end of the road for Big Bob, surely? Bob actually appears on the Sky highlights raising a glass of champagne. England is now, officially, a shiny new nation of Stuart Broads, gambolling fresh-faced into a sunny future. Whither the Old England of Big Bob, a land of righteous anger and weary resignation?

And yet... and yet. Four days later, Willis is back on the horse. Kent v Surrey. Canterbury. "Surrey's bowling was awful, Charles. And their BATTING WAS EVEN WORSE. Chris Adams has got A LOT OF WORK TO DO."

But surely England were off limits? Ashes heroes and all that? Not to Bob.

"I hope England are going to take a reserve opening batsman to South Africa," he rants. "Because they're going to need one. They can't," he snarled, back to his best. "They can't keep picking Alastair Cook WILLY NILLY."

Fellow guest Rob Key tries not to laugh. But it's only funny because it's true, Charles.

GEOFF MILLER

England's National Selector is also a star of the after-dinner circuit. He puts SPIN straight regarding picking players… and comedy

As selectors, the phrase we preach is "consistency and continuity". If that wasn't going to be the case there's no way I'd have taken the job. The days of one in/one out are gone.

When you assess a player there's a sequence of things to look at: first ability, then how big their heart is, and then you talk to them to find out what they've got between the ears.

We try to pick players who can produce on all wickets and in all atmospheres. Occasionally you might, just might, look at a horse for a course. But really you want these blokes to perform all over the world.

The process of selection varies. Sometimes it's face to face, sometimes by video conference. As a selection panel, we see each other very regularly. Our job is to do the miles round the counties, talk to the players, talk to the coaches, umpires, opposition players, the committees…

Selection has to be politically correct. You've got to make sure that no stone is left unturned. You're trying to set up a conveyor belt, so you're looking at peripheral players and younger players as well.

I played for nearly 20 years, including 34 Test matches and all I'm remembered for is catching Jeff Thomson at Melbourne in 1982/83.

There were some good beards in my day, oh yeah. I had one, Brears had one, Mike Hendrick had one; Botham for a while. It all started because we had no running water in Hyderabad, so the lads just said: "Sod it, we'll grow beards for seven days." I kept mine for about eight years.

After-dinner speaking is my main activity: charities, clubs, seminars. I have four or five core stories. People get upset if I don't do them. One line I can use, which people like Ian Botham and Graham Gooch can't, is: "I was rubbish, I was garbage. If anyone

"It's all very loose and self-deprecating. That's the British trend in humour, isn't it?"

watched me play, I apologize now." I just start baggin' myself. It's all very, very loose and self-deprecating. That's the British trend in humour, isn't it?

The biggest lesson I ever learned was: do your homework. I did one for the Barbados tourist industry in London, and I started with a Viv Richards story. It went down like a lead balloon. Then I told them a Michael Holding story. That went down like a lead balloon. I was

sweating cobs. Then I just happened to mention Joel Garner and I realized I'd done Antigua and Jamaica and I hadn't even mentioned Barbados.

I like *Porridge* and *Rising Damp*. Some of the lines are fantastic. You don't pinch those but you glean a kind of method. The modern stuff can be good. Steve Coogan, he's very clever. Vic Reeves as well – silly, but clever.

If you mention Geoff Miller, even to those old enough to have watch the game when I played, they'll say, "Now what era did you play in?" I tell them I roomed with Ian Botham for seven years; he batted six and I batted seven. "I don't remember that," they say. No, I don't expect you do.

BRIAN LARA

The Prince of Trinidad on boyhood heroes, growing up without television and giving something back in the Caribbean

When I was a kid I used to stand in my garage and play with the names of Richards and Greenidge and fit my name in amongst them. So for that to become real was an awesome experience. It was a great honour just to put on the maroon cap, just to be a part of that team.

I like the fact that I'm representing the greatest institution in West Indian life. Cricket has definitely surpassed anything else in the Caribbean. Politics, anything else, doesn't have the same recognition worldwide. From George Headley right through to the present-day players, what cricket has done for us is something that we're all in awe of.

I'm not a bad footballer. Dwight [Yorke] would vouch for me.

Roy Fredericks was my first batting hero. He was the opening batsman in the '70s. Left-handed like myself. Diminutive. Long-sleeved white shirt. He was my first role model and as I got a bit older and understood the game more I appreciated all the West Indies batsmen. Gordon Greenidge for his technique; Desmond Haynes for his fight; Viv Richards for his sheer dominance of the game, the way he was so intimidating. So I learned to take something from everyone and mould them into my own game.

I got into watching the team in the '80s. Television coverage of cricket came in very late in Trinidad. Before that, we had to listen to it on the radio. I'd be up in the middle of the night as a 12-year-old, defying my father's instructions to go to bed, just so that I could listen to the cricket from Australia.

Being captain during the decline of West Indies cricket: of course it had major effects. It's no longer a dream, it's a reality. But it's always been a proud moment whenever I play for the team, it's always been an honour.

I'm happy that kids in the Caribbean have more options these days. There weren't many options in the '70s and '80s when I started, or in the '60s when Viv Richards started. Cricket was the ultimate sport then. It still is the ultimate sport but there's a lot more options for kids now. Not just American sports but opportunities to go to American universities, for example; there's television and cable.

As personalities, we all have a responsibility in the Caribbean. We're not churning out Tiger Woods's and Michael Jordans. The last Trinidadian who was anybody, internationally, before me, was Larry Gomes many years ago. So we are put up on a pedestal, which might be tough. But there are a lot of things you can do as a person to enhance your environment and your community. We're trying our best. Ato Boldon has been an Olympic medallist four times, he does what he has to do when he comes home; Dwight Yorke. No doubt about it, we do take our responsibilities towards the Caribbean community quite seriously.

OLD SCHOOL ASHES

Back in the day, it took England's tourists over two months even to get to Australia. Not to worry: time passed quickly thanks to fancy dress, on-board "rope" golf – and plenty of duty-free fags...

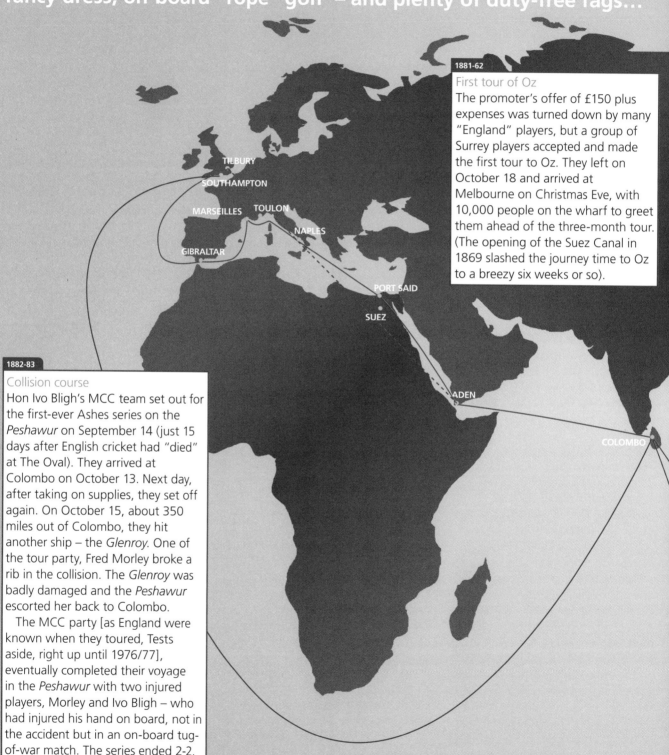

1881-62

First tour of Oz

The promoter's offer of £150 plus expenses was turned down by many "England" players, but a group of Surrey players accepted and made the first tour to Oz. They left on October 18 and arrived at Melbourne on Christmas Eve, with 10,000 people on the wharf to greet them ahead of the three-month tour. (The opening of the Suez Canal in 1869 slashed the journey time to Oz to a breezy six weeks or so).

1882-83

Collision course

Hon Ivo Bligh's MCC team set out for the first-ever Ashes series on the *Peshawur* on September 14 (just 15 days after English cricket had "died" at The Oval). They arrived at Colombo on October 13. Next day, after taking on supplies, they set off again. On October 15, about 350 miles out of Colombo, they hit another ship – the *Glenroy*. One of the tour party, Fred Morley broke a rib in the collision. The *Glenroy* was badly damaged and the *Peshawur* escorted her back to Colombo.

The MCC party [as England were known when they toured, Tests aside, right up until 1976/77], eventually completed their voyage in the *Peshawur* with two injured players, Morley and Ivo Bligh – who had injured his hand on board, not in the accident but in an on-board tug-of-war match. The series ended 2-2.

Map labels: TILBURY, SOUTHAMPTON, MARSEILLES, TOULON, NAPLES, GIBRALTAR, PORT SAID, SUEZ, ADEN, COLOMBO

Glees and songs

England batter Prince Ranjitsinjhi – born abroad and inspirer of a load of merchandise when he came into the England team, rather in the manner of KP – recalled life on board the *Ornuz* for the '97/'98 tourists: "In the afternoons we engaged in cricket practice. In the evenings, the professional members of the team delighted the passengers by singing glees and plantation songs."

On the final leg from Colombo some of the women on board started playing cricket "causing great excitement and merriment among the passengers... At first the ladies showed a very primitive knowledge of cricket… but they improved wonderfully, their bowling and fielding in the end becoming exceedingly smart, although their batting, in most cases, remained comparatively poor." So did England's, as they lost the series 4-1.

Six months on tour

Having sailed on September 24, played in Colombo a month later (hitting 213 to Ceylon's 59), England played the first tour game in Oz on November 10, won the Test series 4-1 and didn't arrive back in London until April 7. Now tell us about modern players' burnout!

Fancy dress

Plum Warner's team also played cricket on board after tea. A team of passengers challenged them to a match: the cricketers won 163 to 31, even though batsmen had to retire at 20. The ship held a fancy dress ball, won by Warner dressed as the "Rajah of Bhong". (Best not ask too much about that, readers.) "We spent our days reading and playing bridge and taking part in deck tournaments. After dinner there was generally a dance or a concert or some sort of amusement," Warner wrote. The preparations obviously worked: England won the series 3-2.

Plotting and planning

St Pancras was packed with fans to give Douglas Jardine and co a huge send-off as his party boarded the boat-train to Tilbury. At stations down the line people waited to catch a glimpse of the players. Another large crowd was at the docks to wish them bon voyage on the SS *Orontes*. It was on the voyage that Jardine outlined his plan of leg theory (or Bodyline) and instructed his side that they were always to refer to Bradman as "the little bastard". Hedley Verity, sailing to Australia for the first time, experimented with new types of deliveries using a tennis ball. When they arrived in Oz, Jardine's team swept the Tests 4-1 in the most controversial Ashes series yet.

The life of Riley

When the SS *Orion* had been out of Southampton some two hours, R.W. V. Robins said: "Well, it's an age since we sailed. We must be very near to Australia now." Australia was still 31 days away. Captain Gubby Allen spent the first three days of the voyage replying to 144 good-luck messages. Deck cricket was again a popular diversion on board although Allen sat it out, having been injured playing it on two previous voyages.

Deck cricket was played with a narrow bat, on a pitch 16 yards long and with a ball covered in rope. Not much bounce off the deck, but the crafty bowler could get "turn" from the roll of the ship. Deck golf was played with a ball attached by rope to a machine that could divine where the shot would have ended up. The chaps also passed time with photography, bridge and dominoes.

Duty free Utopia

The team took on board a slip-catching cradle, and spent an hour-and-a-half each day practising on it. "Although we missed a number of catches early in the tour," reflected Denis Compton, "I always felt that the practice on board the Strathleden paid dividends in the end, because in the Test series England dropped only two possible chances." But to Compton it was the duty-free shop which was the highlight on life on board: "To buy cigarettes at a fifth of their price in England was an entry into Utopia itself."

The last boat trip

The last side to reach its destination by sea, this was also the first MCC side to Australia to leave by air, the team flying to Aden (in Yemen) before joining the *Canberra* for the 10-day voyage to Australia, with a 13-hour stop at Colombo in between. Lord Ted Dexter's team drew the series 1-1 with Richie Benaud's Australians.

PERTH (FREEMANTLE)

ADELAIDE

SYDNEY

MELBOURNE

HOW THE ASHES WERE WON

ENGLAND SURVIVED CARDIFF AND CAME BACK FROM THE HUMILIATION OF LEEDS TO TAKE BACK THE ASHES AT THE OVAL IN A THRILLING ECHO OF 2005. **SPIN** RELIVES 47 FULL-ON DAYS INSIDE THE ASHES BUBBLE

THE GREAT ESCAPE

England got out of jail in Cardiff – and seized momentum in the series

First nPower Test, Cardiff

Fancy seeing you here The 2009 Ashes kicked off on a Wednesday in Wales. Nobody died. The decision to give the game to Sophia Gardens (now 'the SWALEC Stadium'), had attracted criticism from the off and talk that a) the pitch would not be fit for Test cricket or b) it would be a spinners' paradise, perfect for crafty old England. As it happened, Glamorgan's hosting universally praised. The pitch? Well, it was slow and low and did little to encourage positive cricket. But that was all forgotten after a sensational finish…

Clockwise from top left: Welsh songstress Katherine Jenkins kicks things off; Ricky Ponting gets agitated with England 12th man Bilal Shafayat at the death; KP goes exploring outside off-stump and finds only a hapless dismissal and plenty of media criticism. Left: Paul Collingwood's epic second innings 74 saved the Test for England. Opposite page, left: Ricky Ponting became only the second Australian to pass 11,000 Test runs. Right: Marcus North reaches 100, one of an Ashes-record four Aussies to do so in the first innings

Only nearly thrashed The game will surely only be remembered for its sensational last hour when England's last pair – James Anderson and Monty Panesar – heroically kept the Aussies at bay to stave off an innings defeat. It was a cliff-hanger to rival anything

from 2005 and left us confused: it was obvious that the 11 best players in Australia were useful enough to (almost) give England a sound thrashing. But would their failure to apply the killer blow give England – in the buzz-word of the hour – momentum? Either way, the familiar sight of an agitated Ricky Ponting gave England fans something to cheer/jeer and would become one of the recurring themes of the summer.

Kevin Pietersen Puppy murderer. Or so you'd have thought from the criticism following his first-innings dismissal, top edging a sweep to a ball that pitched at least two feet outside off stump. Clearly it wasn't a great shot, but what the critics overlooked was the fact that KP was still England's

top-scorer and the sweep shot brings him many runs. His second innings dismissal – leaving a straight delivery that sent his off stump cartwheeling – hardly won over the critics, either.

Missed opportunity At 228/3, England had an opportunity to set an imposing first innings total. But a glut of poor shot selections cost them and they squandered first use of a flat pitch.

Up to the mark Reports that Ricky Ponting's batting was on the wane were some way off the mark. During the course of his sublime century, Ponting became just the second man to pass 11,000 Test runs for Australia (after Allan Border). It was the third time he had scored a century in the first innings of an Ashes series and

"I was unfortunate to hit the ball into my helmet. If that hadn't happened, I'd have got away with it"

KP counters criticism of Day 1 horror-shot

Above, left: Jimmy Anderson and Monty Panesar defied Australia for a nailbiting 69 balls in a series-defining last-wicket stand. Above right and opposite: Aussie players and fans cheer Brad Haddin's second Test ton, as the tourists push on for a first innings lead of 239. Top right and opposite: Brad Haddin and Michael Clarke walk out on the third evening, as Test cricket is played under lights in England for the first time

underlined that his determination not to experience a repeat of 2005 was a strong motivating force.

Hidden depths Australia bat deep. Not only did four of them score centuries in their only innings – the first time they've done that in the Ashes – but two of them were batting at six and seven. But England's tail also wagged. In the first innings, their last two wickets added 80; in the second they saved the game.

Two spinners England's policy of playing two spinners and exploiting a turning pitch didn't work at all. Not only was the turn slow and grudging,

but neither Swann or Panesar were at their best. Australia's Nathan Hauritz, to everyone's surprise, looked the best spinner in the match.

Reliant on Flintoff Anderson and, in particular, Stuart Broad, endured poor games with the ball, meaning Flintoff bowled more overs than either of them. Though he tired, his first spell was irresistible and accounted for Phil Hughes, softened up by the short ball. When the ball doesn't swing, England looked dispiritingly toothless.

New faces Of the Australian seamers, it was Peter Siddle and Ben Hilfenhaus who impressed most of all. Siddle

bowled with pace, discipline and aggression – giving Swann a real battering – while Hilfenhaus swung the ball at a sharp pace.

Glovegate With Anderson and Panesar resisting grimly on the last evening, England tried to buy time by sending on the 12th man – Bilal Shafayat – with a fresh pair of gloves and a drink for Anderson. Though that was reluctantly accepted by the Aussies, Shafayat's reappearance at the end of the next over – this time with the physio – was less welcome. England claimed that Anderson had spilt water over his fresh gloves and so required a third pair. Ponting was unconvinced.

> "I didn't see anyone call for the physio to come out. As far as I'm concerned, it was pretty ordinary, really"
>
> *Ricky Ponting, wound up after England's "time-wasting" on Day 5*

Saved Anderson and Panesar clung on for 69 balls on the last day to secure the draw – and possibly, ultimately, to win England the series. When they came together, England still needed six to make Australia bat again. Though Anderson and Panesar made the headlines for the heart-in-mouth finale, it was Paul Collingwood's six-hour 74 that had been key. The result also raised questions about Ponting's tactics: Hilfenhaus, easily the best bowler, was strangely under-bowled, with Ponting using the out-of-sorts Johnson and the part-time spin of North. In truth, though, England's survival just underlined how much Australia missed Shane Warne.

SCOREBOARD

TOSS WON BY: ENGLAND

FIRST nPOWER TEST, CARDIFF, JULY 8–12
ENGLAND 435 all out
(Pietersen 69, Collingwood 64, Prior 56, Swann 46*) and 252/9

AUSTRALIA 674/6 dec
(Ponting 150, North 125*, Katich 122, Haddin 121) Match drawn

ENGLAND 0
AUSTRALIA 0
Man of the match: **Ricky Ponting**

36
Number of runs per wicket scored by England

· · · · · · · · · · · ·

112
Number of runs per wicket scored by Australia

· · · · · · · · · · · ·

69
Balls faced by last pair Monty Panesar and Jimmy Anderson to save the match

· · · · · · · · · · · ·

1
Times England have won the first Test in the last 15 series

· · · · · · · · · · · ·

10
Estimated value, in millions of pounds, of the Test to the Cardiff economy

ENGLAND BREAK HQ HOODOO

How England beat the Aussies at Lord's for the first time in 75 years

Second nPower Test, Lords

Right from the off England – following on from Cardiff – seemed to have the momentum in their favour at Lord's: Andrew Strauss won the toss, batted and went to lunch at 126/0 off 29 overs. A dream start. Maybe it was pure momentum; maybe it was the skipper playing on his home ground; or maybe it was – simply – that Australia's fast bowlers, particularly Mitchell Johnson, were in such indifferent form. None of them had played at Lord's before: Johnson – already struggling at Cardiff, without a slope – bowled short and wide. His

eight overs went for 53 in the first session, including 11 of the 22 boundaries hit. Ricky Ponting's body language, not for the first time, often appeared to be saying, "What have the selectors sent me?" as he dreamed of the bygone control of Glenn McGrath – or even the sidelined Stuart Clark.

England brought in Graham Onions for Monty Panesar. Steve Harmison, having knocked over Phil Hughes twice for the England Lions, became unignorable once there was a doubt over Flintoff's fitness. But Harmison,

named in the squad, was overlooked for the XI in favour of Durham team-mate Onions, who had helped introduce the Flower-Strauss era with his five-for on debut against the Windies in May. As it happened, Onions bowled just 20 overs in the game – compared to Jimmy Anderson's 42, Andrew Flintoff's 39 and Stuart Broad's 34.

Was this Andrew Flintoff's last Test? Flintoff's years-long struggle with injuries was well documented but, even so, the announcement of his retirement from Test cricket after the

Opposite: Andrew Flintoff cleans up Peter Siddle on the last day to clinch his first Test five-for at Lord's. This page, clockwise from top left: Flintoff and England celebrate on the last day; Graeme Swann wraps up victory; another bad Test at the office for the mojo-less Mitchell Johnson; Andrew Strauss leaves the stage after his 161

Ashes on the eve of the Lord's Test came as a shock. Ricky Ponting wondered if a farewell circus would distract England but the news merely ensured a standing ovation for Flintoff every time he appeared, raising the volume of a Lord's crowd not always known for their vocal support. As he left the field after pretty much every over (ish), talk was that this Test might be his swansong. Flintoff, though, was hoping for an Oval goodbye.

The English disease Australia's collapse in the first innings was largely their own fault: Hughes flicked at a wide

one down leg-side from Anderson; Hussey left one from Flintoff and was bowled; Haddin and Johnson, inexplicably, hooked Broad straight to men in the deep. And Punter Ponting? Well, he wasn't caught – which was what was given – but he *was* lbw. Either way, he wasn't happy. Which made the English crowd, whose goading and booing of the irascible Aussie skip was a big feature here, very very happy.

Should Strauss have enforced the follow-on? England were 210 ahead on first innings but Strauss – possibly

Andrew Strauss' fourth Test century at Lord's carried on the momentum seized on the last day at Cardiff

mindful of Flintoff's potential fragility, opted to bat again. It did nothing to win over those who regard him as an overly defensive captain and on the Saturday afternoon, when England's premier stroke-makers Bopara and Pietersen took 119 balls to put on 50, it seemed that England were losing that momentum. Collingwood and Prior (61 off 42 balls) picked things up, allowing an overnight declaration: Australia needed 522 to win, with two days to play.

Ponting's men were playing against 13 Or could have been forgiven for thinking so. Setting out on their record pursuit on Sunday morning, three of the first four wickets to fall were as a result of highly dubious decisions: Katich was caught off a Flintoff no-ball, Hughes was "caught" by Strauss, diving forward in the slips, though replays suggested he might well have scooped it up on the bounce; Hussey was "caught" at slip off a sharply turning Swann ball that missed the bat

> *"We just have to bounce back.
> We've got a tour game now to rectify
> a few things that were glaringly
> obvious here with the ball"*
>
> *Punter, hoping to improve his bowlers,
> since he can't improve the umpires*

Alastair Cook's 95 would prove to be the only time he passed 50 in a disappointing series

43

Number of runs per wicket
scored by England

. . . .

30

Number of runs per wicket
scored by Australia

. . . .

51

Number of Test innings James
Anderson has had without a
duck – a record

. . . .

36.22

Michael Clarke's Test average
when he was dropped in 2006

. . . .

52.36

Clarke's average since his recall
for the 2006 Ashes

completely. Only Ponting's dismissal, played on to Stuart Broad, appeared legitimate. But even after all that, the Aussies still weren't beaten.

It all got a little twitchy on the Sunday evening Michael Clarke and Brad Haddin batted unbeaten throughout the final session, taking the score from the down-and-out 178/5 at tea to the could-they-do-it 313/5 at close. Had we all forgotten Sri Lanka hitting 537/9 to save the game in the last innings at Lord's in 2006? Or South Africa losing just three wickets in ten hours' batting as they saved the Test in 2008? If Cardiff had been Old Trafford 2005 in reverse, all the talk was of Lord's becoming a carbon copy of Edgbaston 2005.

It didn't happen The game was wrapped up ten minutes short of lunch on the fifth day, as Flintoff produced an inspirational spell of fast bowling – touching speeds of 93mph, as fast as any Englishman in living memory. He removed Haddin with the fourth ball of his first over of the morning; Haddin hanging his bat out

at a good length, quick delivery. But it took golden-arm Graeme Swann, coming on for the 13th over of the morning, to remove Clarke, with a drifting, slower-ball full toss that beat the Aussie in the flight. Clarke, having played one of the great innings, left the field. With him went any hope of a miraculous Australian victory.

SCOREBOARD
TOSS WON BY: ENGLAND

SECOND nPOWER TEST, LORDS, JULY 16–20
ENGLAND 425 all out (Strauss 161, Cook 95, Hilfenhaus 4/103) & 311/6d (Prior 61, Collingwood 54)

AUSTRALIA 215 all out (Hussey 51, Anderson 4/55) & 406 all out (Clarke 136, Haddin 80, Johnson 63, Flintoff 5/92). ENGLAND won by 115 runs

ENGLAND 1
AUSTRALIA 0
Man of the match: **Andrew Flintoff**

WEATHER HAS LAST WORD

England's chances are washed away in Birmingham – but, still one-down, it's the Aussies who most rue the grim Brum climate

Third nPower Test, Edgbastion

Working all night It had rained nearly every day in Birmingham over the fortnight preceding the Test and there were serious doubts as to whether the game would be staged at all. As it happened, we lost the equivalent of nearly two days' play – the damage-limitation achieved by groundstaff working through the night throughout the game, mopping up and getting things as close to playable as humanly possible. Though England, briefly, had a chance of springing a surprise win in the shortened game, there was a

definite sense that, one-up, if it rained until September, Strauss and co would not be all that unhappy.

Punter gets it right Four years ago, after plenty of pre-match rain and the suggestion of assistance for the fast bowlers, Ricky Ponting won the toss here, put England in and saw his McGrath-less attack concede 390 – and the momentum in the series. This time, the Aussies again succumbed to

a surprise late injury: while McGrath had trodden on a ball, keeper Brad Haddin broke a finger in the warm-up, leading to a debut for reserve gloveman Graham Manou. But Ponting did not repeat his own mishap, winning the toss for the only time in the series and electing to bat. He got that right: the pitch was lifeless, and Australia finished at 126/1, from the 30 overs that were possible towards the end of the opening day.

Opposite: Marcus North fell short of a third century in his fifth Test – but his 96 helped secure the draw for the Aussies. Andrew MacDonald and Mitchell Johnson try to escape the rain on the washed-out Saturday. By the final day, Andrew Flintoff is visibly ailing – but still bowled a seven-over spell in a forlorn search for the breakthrough. Above: Graham Onions removes Shane Watson and Mr Cricket Mike Hussey with his first two balls of Day 2 – and catches the eye of miniature pop minx Lily Allen, amongst others

"New Bradman" not good enough Manou aside, the biggest story of the opening day was Phil Hughes' axing: the Aussie wonder boy had come to the series on the back of prodigious, Bradman-esque scores in his debut series in South Africa (and in his county stint for Middlesex at the start of the summer) but had looked less than certain against the short ball at Cardiff and Lord's.

Onions chops through tourists Hughes' replacement, the makeshift opener Shane Watson, started well: he and Simon Katich put on 85 (the highest partnership in the innings) in their first Test stand together. For England, the only bright spot of the opening day was Swann trapping

Katich leg before. Graham Onions collected a double strike, from his first two balls of Day 2, with Watson adjudged leg before and Mr Cricket Mike Hussey – not for the only time in the series – fatally misjudging a leave only to see his stumps go flying. Onions' breakthroughs gained him the interest of pint-sized popette Lily Allen, who wonders on Twitter if he is single. His day got better, as he removed Ricky Ponting, just after he'd taken the title of Australia's all-time leading Test run scorer. Australia could have done with more of those runs: Ponting was out for 38, as seven wickets fell quickly, leaving a disappointing final total of 263. At stumps on Day 2, England were 116/2 and eyeing the possibility of a first innings lead.

Ben Hilfenhaus took four in the first innings and was Australia's leading wicket-taker in the series. Opposite: The equivalent of nearly two full days was lost to rain at Edgbaston

Just a glimpse for England It was Andrew Flintoff, on his farewell tour, that prospered when play resumed on the Sunday – he bashed a 79-ball 74 while Ian Bell and Stuart Broad pitched in with 50s. Australia faced a deficit of 113, with a nervy day-and-a-bit remaining; the nerves jangled a little louder once Onions' swing had accounted for Katich, and Swann had spun one through Ponting's defence. With the tourists two-down and 25 runs behind at the close, it seemed that that, without the rain, England could have gone 2-0 up in the series. And maybe still could…

The end of the road for Fred? Michael Clarke followed up his brilliant Lord's ton with another innings to spare the Aussies any jitters. Coming in at a still-in-the-balance 137/3, Clarke batted for four hours 41 minutes of the final day, his partnership of 185 with Marcus North taking Australia to safety. England's hopes of quick wickets weren't helped by what appeared to be a half-fit Flintoff hobbling around the field; with the game obviously meandering to a draw, Strauss threw the ball to Ravi Bopara and Paul Collingwood, to spare Flintoff. The Fred Fitness Watch, already in full swing after Lord's, goes into overdrive even before the Edgbaston draw was official. Would *this* be his last Test? The stalemate means England head into the fourth Test in an even better position than in 2005; with a series lead to protect.

DRYJOYS

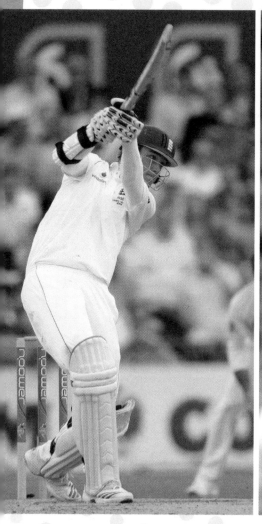

ENGLAND HUMBLED

Shambolic England are beaten within two-and-a-half days, Ashes hopes apparently ground into dust by resurgent Aussies

Fourth nPower Test, Headingley
As you were England had been telling themselves that they they had the measure of this Australian team. But at Leeds, normal service was resumed. England looked shambolic, inept; Australia looked like world-beaters. The tourists levelled the series with an innings win inside two-and-a-half days and most sensible opinion felt that, after this, there was no way back for England – or at least not unless they turned to one of the stars of yesteryear, as a media cry for the return of Mark Ramprakash and Marcus Trescothick went up.

Three jeers for the middle-order If Ricky Ponting was getting booed at Lord's, the chances of convincing the Leeds crowd to lay off the Australian skipper were slim. Yet ECB Chairman Giles Clarke tried anyway, urging the Headingley crowd not to boo Punter on his walk to and from the wicket. His pleas went unheeded, but if anyone warranted jeers it was England's middle order.

Poor preparation Australia romped back into the series on the back of a very one-sided first day: that saw England, having won the toss, slump to 72/6 at lunch, and finally rolled over for 102 inside 34 overs. England's haplessness started early. Evacuated from their hotel at 5am thanks to a fire alarm, they also suffered a last-minute injury crisis, on top of Flintoff's confirmed absence, as Matt Prior suffered back spasms during a warm-up game of football. Australia agreed to delay the toss, while England did fitness Tests on their gloveman and pondered the availability of emergency replacements. At one point Paul Collingwood was seen with the gloves and even names like Alec Stewart and Bruce French were mentioned.

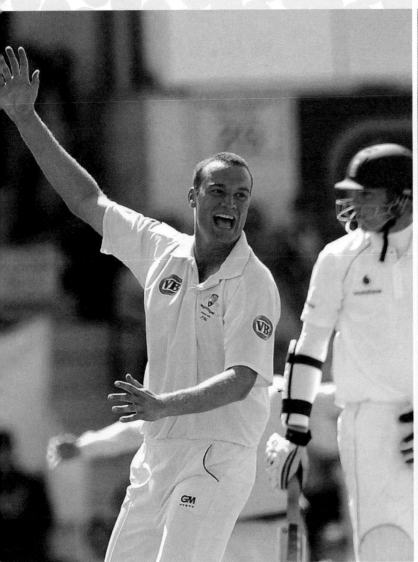

From far left: Stuart Broad's 61 from 49 balls in the second innings came too late to save England; Marcus North's stunning reflex catch removes Andrew Strauss on the first morning and starts the rot; the recalled Stuart Clark picked up three wickets on the first morning to leave England 72/6 at lunch; Ravi Bopara – out for 1 and 0 – played his last Test for a while, after two more failures; skipper Strauss takes stock at the end of the innings thrashing. Below: a resurgent Mitchell Johnson cleaned up Ian Bell in both innings

Eventually, Prior took his place in the XI, and top-scored with 37.

33.5 overs of pain Finally, Australia bowled like Australia. The match saw the (belated) return of Stuart Clark – the leading wicket-taker in the 2006/7 series, despite being in a squad boasting McGrath and Warne – as selectors finally decided he was ready for Test cricket again. He picked up just where he left off, with 3/18. Mitchell Johnson not only landed the ball on the pitch, but also remembered how to bowl his in-ducker. England's middle order were all rolled for single figure scores in both innings.
On the bright side for the hosts, the disastrous innings lasted three balls longer than the innings of 51 against the West Indies in Jamaica.

Short and wide and badly Still, in conditions offering a bit for bowlers, England – especially given Australia's recent history of collapses – would have fancied their chances of staying in it, provided they bowled well. They didn't: they bowled short and wide and badly and there was no hiding the frustration on the faces of Strauss and Flower. After just one day of play,

ENGLAND 1st Inns 102

AUSTRALIA 1st Inns

Far left, above: Marcus North celebrates his second century of the series, as Australia take a lead of 343. Far left, below: Hilfenhaus removes Strauss in the second innings. Left: Peter Siddle's 5/21 was the outstanding performance of the match. Above: Matt Prior receives help after his pre-match back spasm

Australia already had a first-innings lead of 94 runs, with Shane Watson scoring a third 50 as opener. Their scoring rate eliminated any hope of an England fightback – they scored a four an over early on the second day, leaving England needing 344 just to make the tourists bat again with still three and a bit days left in the Test. A hopeful start of 58/0 was soon ruined, with Australia claiming five wickets – including the dubious lbw of Ravi Bopara – in the last half-hour. A win inside two days seemed possible.

Shifting momentum England managed to avoid that particular humiliation. In the morning, Stuart Broad (61) and Graeme Swann (62) had a swing of the bat – free in the knowledge the match was gone. It did take until after lunch for the result to be sealed, but that was little consolation for England, who had succumbed to a decent, but far from imperfect, Australian attack. Momentum was with the tourists as the sides headed back to London.

77
Tests since England had gone into a Test without either Andrew Flintoff or Kevin Pietersen

40.21
Stuart Broad's Test bowling average coming into the game

3
Official ICC world ranking of Australia's Stuart Clark, ignored for first three games of the series

16
Total runs scored in the match by England's Nos 3-5 – Ravi Bopara, Ian Bell and Paul Collingwood – an English record

7
Number of Tests played by Steve Harmison, out of 28, since June 2007, before his comeback here

SCOREBOARD
TOSS WON BY: ENGLAND

FOURTH nPOWER TEST, HEADINGLEY, AUGUST 7–9
ENGLAND 102 (Siddle 5/21) and 263 (Swann 62, Broad 61, Johnson 5/69, Hilfenhaus 4/60)

AUSTRALIA 445 (North 110, Clarke 93, Ponting 78, Watson 51, Broad 6/91) Australia won by an innings and 80 runs

ENGLAND 1
AUSTRALIA 1
Man of the match: Michael North

THE ASHES COME HOME

Sixty minutes of magic from Broad and a debut ton from Trott spring surprise glory for written-off England

Fifth nPower Test, Brit Oval

A gloomy forecast The fortnight since the Leeds thrashing had been packed with speculation of mass changes: Mark Ramprakash, Marcus Trescothick, Rob Key were all offered as solutions to England's plywood top/middle-order issues. In the end, the selectors made just one change, sending the shell-shocked Ravi Bopara back to county cricket and calling in Jonathan Trott, who had been in the party at Leeds. Trott had risen almost without trace but, as one of the five men in

the world to average 40-plus in all forms of the game, had earned his chance through sheer weight of county runs. His second innings 119 would be only the second century by an Ashes debutant in over 100 years.

England's chance "gone" Leaving out the spinner Hauritz – a decision the selectors admitted in hindsight was a big mistake – Australia apparently enjoyed a good first day, despite Ponting calling incorrectly once again: at close England were 307/8, largely

Clockwise from top left: Andrew Strauss won his fourth, and possibly most important, toss of the series; Peter Siddle wheeled out his raging celebration four times on Day 1, as England "slumped", or so we thought, to 307/8; Stuart Broad's wonder spell on the Friday - four wickets for eight runs in 21 balls – decided the Ashes; while fourth day run-outs of Michael Clarke (by Andrew Strauss) and Ricky Ponting (by Andrew Flintoff) cemented England's advantage. Jonathan Trott's 119 was only the second Ashes debut century in over 100 years

7.5m
Viewing figures for finale of 2005 Ashes on Channel 4 (on a Monday)

. . . .

1.9m
Viewing figures for finale of 2009 Ashes on Sky Sports (on a Sunday)

. . . .

34.15
Average runs per wicket scored by England during the series

. . . .

40.64
Average runs per wicket scored by Australia

. . . .

331
Length, in minutes, of Trott's ton – 46 minutes longer than KP's Ashes-winning 158 from 2005

The final countdown (clockwise from top left)… Matt Prior stumps Marcus North, Steve Harmison celebrates two wickets in two balls, Graeme Swann removes Mr Cricket Mike Hussey – and the skipper gets his hands on the urn

thanks to a hundred partnership between Andrew Strauss (55) and Bell (72). The afternoon saw a familiar collapse – Trott run out unluckily, Flintoff wafting airily – and on a wicket that most pundits see as a batsman's paradise, almost everyone thought that England's chance had gone.

Broad wins the Ashes An hour of magic from Stuart Broad changed all that. Shortly after a Friday lunch break extended by – possibly vital – rain, Broad came on with Australia 66/0. Shane Watson welcomed him with a thumping drive for four. Yet Broad struck back, catching Watson leg

before in the same over to spark a dramatic collapse that ended up deciding the Ashes. Broad looked a different bowler. Pitching it up on a good length and getting some movement, he took four wickets for eight runs, in just 21 balls and The Brit Oval was in uproar. Australia avoided the follow-on, but 172 behind in a low-scoring game looked conclusive.

An impossible chase? But with England you never can tell. They lost three quick wickets before stumps on the second day and when, off the first ball of the third day, the raging Siddle was adamant he'd had Trott caught

behind, English hearts were pumping. Could there be a final twist? Well... no. Ponting soon turned to his innocuous spinners and England, slowly but surely, began to compile a total that would set up a massive total for Australia to pursue. Ponting, hit by Prior while fielding at short leg, spent the third afternoon wondering whether his bleeding mouth was hurting him more than the nail-in-coffin slogging of Graeme Swann, who added 63 within an hour of Trott's nerveless, steady scoring. The eventual target, 546, is well beyond any achieved in Test history. But Australia's solid start (80/0 at the close) had nervous bookmakers offering ridiculously short odds on a surprise victory.

The breakthrough Swann and Broad removed an opener each in the first hour of the last day. Even so, there was no sign of the calamitous collapse of the first dig, as Ricky Ponting and Mike Hussey, after a grim series, mounted a slow and steady charge at the total. Paul Collingwood missed a sharp chance off Ponting but, apart from that, Strauss later conceded that, for a time, he had no idea where his next wicket was coming from. Into the afternoon session, Australia were 217/2. Called for a risky single, Ponting was doomed when Andrew Flintoff

pegged down the stumps from mid-on. Pandemonium. Michael Clarke soon follows, the victim of an unlucky rebound off short leg Alastair Cook to Strauss at leg slip, who ran him out.

The home stretch Despite the ongoing attempts of Mr Cricket Mike Hussey to hold the Aussie tail together, the series-long tension finally lifted, as it became clear to the crowd and players that it would be Andrew Strauss lifting the urn. There was just time for Steve Harmison to roar in and help mop up the tail – he took the eighth and ninth wickets in consecutive balls before Graeme Swann sealed the victory – as he had at Lord's – removing Hussey at 5:53pm. The Ashes were back.

THE STATS

Batting ENGLAND

	M	I	NO	Runs	HS	Ave	SR	100/50
IJL Trott	1	2	0	160	119	80.00	58.39	1/0
AJ Strauss	5	9	0	474	161	52.66	49.84	1/3
KP Pietersen	2	4	0	153	69	38.25	49.67	0/1
GP Swann	5	8	1	249	63	35.57	83.27	0/2
A Flintoff	4	7	1	200	74	33.33	72.72	0/1
MJ Prior	5	9	1	261	61	32.62	81.81	0/2
SJ Harmison	2	3	2	31	19*	31.00	67.39	0/0
SCJ Broad	5	9	1	234	61	29.25	72.67	0/2
IR Bell	3	5	0	140	72	28.00	47.29	0/2
PD Collwood	5	9	0	250	74	27.77	40.65	0/3
AN Cook	5	9	0	222	95	24.66	52.11	0/1
JM Anderson	5	8	2	99	29	16.50	55.30	0/0
RS Bopara	4	7	0	105	35	15.00	46.05	0/0
MS Panesar	1	2	1	11	7*	11.00	21.15	0/0
G Onions	3	4	2	19	17*	9.50	37.25	0/0

Batting AUSTRALIA

	M	I	NO	Runs	HS	Ave	SR	100/50
MJ Clarke	5	8	1	448	136	64.00	57.43	2/2
MJ North	5	8	1	367	125*	52.42	49.86	2/1
RT Ponting	5	8	0	385	150	48.12	66.26	1/2
SR Watson	3	5	0	240	62	48.00	54.91	0/3
BJ Haddin	4	6	0	278	121	46.33	69.50	1/1
SM Katich	5	8	0	341	122	42.62	53.87	1/1
MEK Hussey	5	8	0	276	121	34.50	47.83	1/2
NM Hauritz	3	3	1	45	24	22.50	49.45	0/0
GA Manou	1	2	1	21	13*	21.00	53.84	0/0
B Hilfenhaus	5	6	4	40	20	20.00	49.38	0/0
PJ Hughes	2	3	0	57	36	19.00	58.76	0/0
PM Siddle	5	6	0	91	35	18.20	65.46	0/0
MG Johnson	5	6	0	105	63	17.50	62.13	0/1
SR Clark	2	3	0	38	32	12.66	122.58	0/0

Bowling

	O	M	R	W	BB	Ave	Econ	SR
SCJ Broad	154.1	25	544	18	6/91	30.22	3.52	51.3
G Onions	77.4	11	303	10	4/58	30.30	3.90	46.6
SJ Harmison	43.0	10	167	5	3/54	33.40	3.88	51.6
GP Swann	170.2	30	567	14	4/38	40.50	3.32	73.0
JM Anderson	158.0	38	542	12	5/80	45.16	3.43	79.0
A Flintoff	128.5	18	417	8	5/92	52.12	3.23	96.6
PD Colw'ood	18.0	1	76	1	1/38	76.00	4.22	108.0
MS Panesar	35.0	4	115	1	1/115	115.00	3.28	210.0
RS Bopara	8.2	1	44	0	-	-	-	-

Bowling

	O	M	R	W	BB	Ave	Econ	SR
B Hilfenhaus	180.5	40	604	22	4/60	27.45	3.34	49.3
PM Siddle	161.4	24	616	20	5/21	30.80	3.81	48.5
NM Hauritz	103.2	17	321	10	3/63	32.10	3.10	62.0
MG Johnson	162.1	15	651	20	5/69	32.55	4.01	48.6
SR Clark	47.0	12	176	4	3/18	44.00	3.74	70.5
MJ North	67.3	13	204	4	4/98	51.00	3.02	101.2
MJ Clarke	19.0	1	75	1	1/12	75.00	3.94	114.0
SM Katich	10.0	2	27	0	-	-	2.70	-
SR Watson	8.0	0	49	0	-	-	6.12	-

Flintoff celebrates removing Simon Katich. He is in the middle of bowling unchanged throughout the morning of the fourth day of the final Ashes Test. Flintoff finishes with 5/78 from 34 overs. He is England's leading wicket-taker as they reclaim the Ashes; only Trescothick and Pietersen score more runs

END OF AN ERA

Andrew Flintoff's inspirational 11-year Test career finished this summer. SPIN salutes one of English cricket's icons

Brit Oval, September 12, 2005
Celebrating with Steve Harmison and a Beefy-esque cigar after England have recaptured the Ashes for the first time in 18 years. Despite having made his Test debut in 1998, the 2005 series is, largely as a result of injuries, Flintoff's first Ashes. Nevertheless, he is England's man of the series

Marriott Hotel, Heathrow, October 6 2006
Flintoff addresses the press on the eve of
his first full winter as captain. Sidelined
with an ankle injury, he has not played
for England for four months. The winter
will see his side whitewashed in the Ashes
and Flintoff himself disciplined over the
"Fredalo incident", in which he had to be
rescued after falling from a pedalo during
the World Cup in the West Indies

RIGHT Edgbaston, August 6 2005
Acknowledging the crowd after bringing up his 50 with a six off Michael Kasprowicz. Flintoff is in the middle of a series-turning innings, hitting 73 off 86 balls, as he puts on 51 for the last wicket with Simon Jones. Later in the afternoon, he will remove Justin Langer and Ricky Ponting in what many will regard as the perfect over

RIGHT Trent Bridge, August 26 2005
Hitting out on the second day of the fourth Ashes Test, on his way to 102 from 132 balls. It is Flintoff's fifth Test century – and his last before announcing his retirement nearly four years later. Even so, just four players in Test history have hit more sixes than Flintoff (82), and none of them Englishmen

FAR LEFT Perth, December 18 2006
Flintoff's England have just lost the Ashes, their chase of 557 to save the series having ended in defeat by 206 runs. England will lose the series 5-0, their first Ashes whitewash since 1921

ABOVE LEFT Trent Bridge, July 22 1998
On the eve of his Test debut, the 20-year-old Flintoff speaks with his Lancashire and England team-mate Michael Atherton. Flintoff will be dropped after two Tests bring a return of two ducks, 17 runs and one wicket for 110. He will not return to the Test side until November 1999

LEFT Mumbai, March 19 2006
Fans show their affection, as the larger-than-life Flintoff inspires England to his only Test win as captain, levelling the series with India 1-1

LIVE FROM THE STREATHAM WETHERSPOONS...

An A–Z (okay, B–W) of the **SPIN** podcast. It's No 3 on iTunes, of course

Blofeld, Henry. Test Match Special gantryist. Does his own podcast and is apparently, in all seriousness, v keen to come down the Wetherspoons and sit in the fourth seat (qv). We'll see.

Brains. Nickname of friend of Colin the Janitor (qv), who left job at Croydon library because he'd read all the books and had nothing left to read. Brains' other nickname is, rather cumbersomely, "Encyclopaedia Britannica". The Janitor maintains this is a true story. But it can't be. Can it?

Building for the future. Ruinous and inexplicable policy pursued by some sports coaches, eg Mr Excitement Duncan Fletcher and Professor Wenger. The Third Umpire writes: "What's so special about the future? Are they putting up the prize money? What's wrong with trying to win something this year?"

Cure for cancer. "If I found a cure for cancer, I'd still be known as the guy that ran out Ricky Ponting," averred Gary Pratt. (Since then, Gary has decided to abandon his medical research. Happy now?)

Discipline, pain of. "The pain of discipline is nothing compared to the pain of failure." Aussie vice-skip Michael Clarke has an Arabic translation of this quote – devised by hardcore ex-team-mate Alfie Langer – tattooed on his arm. You?

Flintoff, Andrew. Appeared in episode 5 of the podcast, talking about his morning radio habits. While Fred was a fan of Wogan, he had little time for Sarah Kennedy or Ken Bruce. As a result he had now started giving Smooth FM a go, though was concerned that "they seem to only have about five CDs".

Fourth seat. Spare seat round podcast table still available for anyone who's keen.

Franz Ferdinand. Art rockers who were remixing their album (or something) in the building next to SPIN HQ. This is true. We saw the singer (old Franz himself) in the street many times but never managed to

Hear the **SPIN** podcast, with star interviews, pin-sharp punditry and so-so comedy at spincricket.com and via itunes

mention it on the podcast, even when we claimed that Colin the Janitor was going to read his Iceland Christmas shopping receipt over an art rock soundtrack for our Christmas special. Missed opportunity all round.

Hannon, Neil. Popster who released much-praised cricket-themed album, the Duckworth-Lewis Method, in the summer of 2009. Special edition of the podcast with Neil picked up our highest-ever audience, if you care.

ICC Awards: Nadir of all broadcast television. See also "ICC Cricket World", below.

ICC Cricket World: Other nadir of all broadcast television. Production values make the National Lottery Show seem like *The Matrix*. Features abnormally high number of still images and a voiceover by a fellow who is apparently a stranger to a) cricket and b) speaking English, which is surely c) a problem when doing the voiceover for an English-language cricket show. Still.

The Imperial. World War I-themed bar in London SE1. Mooted future home of podcast. More upmarket than the 'Spoons (qv). THE place to go for London's in-crowd. Don't wait til the *Guardian* tells you about it before you go – it'll be too late then.

Janitor, Colin the. By media law, all cricket podcasts must include at least one person of pensionable age.

Hear exclusive podcast material from the **SPIN** team including an interview with Freddie Flintoff at spincricket.com

Technically, this is meant to be Tony Greig or Ian Chappell or similar. But we've flouted the spirit of the law by having the **SPIN** janitor come on and share the benefits of his wisdom. So.

Models, non-linear stock market forecast.
SPIN to Andrew Strauss, September 2006: "Do you have a secret talent?"
Strauss: "I've got a great interest in non-linear economic stock market forecasting models.
SPIN: "Is that true?"
Strauss: "Yeah – chaos theory to predict future trends in the stock market. It's not a GREAT interest. But I've read a couple of books on it."

So there you have it.

Number three. Where the **SPIN** podcast is – famously – in the itunes Cricket Podcast charts.

"Pleasing". How Michael Vaughan described the birth of his first daughter; also how Stuart Broad described the winning of the Ashes. Not how **SPIN** was tempted to describe wearying modern obsession with media training.

Prawn, Giant. Asked to prove he was Australian in episode 10, Jono Russell said: "I come from a town where the main attraction is the big prawn." Well, you can Google "Ballina Prawn" and see what he's talking about. It's worth it, sort of.

Richard, Sir Cliff. "I didn't mind his early records but I can't say anything he's done since 1965 has moved me either way": Bob Willis, **SPIN** issue 2.

Sidhu. Genius Indian commentator, phrase-maker and erstwhile **SPIN** columnist: "The Indian selectors have

a policy of, 'If it ain't broke, break it.'" Statistics are like mini-skirts: they hide more than they reveal." And so on. "He's very entertaining… but I'm not sure that's what people want from commentary," one Sky gantryist observed to **SPIN**, weirdly.

Slippers. England's winning the CB Series after losing the 2006/07 Ashes 5-0 was "like winning a pair of slippers after having your legs amputated", according to **SPIN**'s own George Dobell.

St Pancras. Mark Butcher – patron saint of the **SPIN** podcast – appeared on the big TV screen in the Streatham Wetherspoons, during a recording of the **SPIN** podcast. Like being in St Pancras station and seeing St Pancras.

Streatham Wetherspoons. Home of the podcast.

Underpants. "Life without sport is like life without underpants," Billy Bowden, **SPIN** issue 10.

Woolworths. What made Sir Richard Hadlee into a fast bowler, according to the man himself in podcast episode six. (True – working there was his first-ever job and it taught him a lot about discipline, attention to detail, you get the picture.)

2010: 9 THINGS WE CAN'T WAIT TO SEE

Dale Steyn: "If this doesn't bamboozle England, maybe my 92-mph outswingers will"

Adam Gilchrist: still a world-beater in the parallel universe of IPL

SOUTH AFRICA v ENGLAND

When: November 2009 to January 2010
Where: South Africa

Will England come back to Earth with a big old bump against the team ranked No 1 in both the Test and ODI forms of the game? Can anyone replace Flintoff? Will the cheery Saffer crowds give Jonathan Trott the same super-nice welcome they always give Kevin Pietersen?

In 2005, England's 2-1 win in South Africa proved they had what it took to take on the all-conquering Aussies that summer. But whereas the 2005 Ashes success came on the back of five series wins in a row, the 2009 triumph came out of the blue, after a year in which South Africa, India and West Indies had all given England what-for. No open-top buses this time: Andy Flower knows that winning the Ashes is very much the start of the journey to being the world No 1. The Saffers beat England 2-1 in England in 2008, going on to be the first team to win a series in Australia for 16 years. Reasons to be hopeful? Well, come the start of the series on November 24, the Saffers won't have played a Test for nine months. And that's the best we can offer.

Key man? Likely to be Saffer fast bowler (and SPIN columnist) Dale Steyn, ranked the world's No 1 Test bowler. He's taken 119 Test wickets at 20 each in the last two years at a strike rate of 36. Didn't fire on the England tour in 2008. Will England get off lightly twice?

IPL

When: March 12 to April 26
Where: India

The third edition of cricket's richest tournament starts a month earlier than usual to accommodate the ICC World Twenty20 – and, with England not playing in this period, we should see a more whole-hearted involvement from stars like Flintoff and Kevin Pietersen who were limited to part-time roles in 2009.

Whether IPL franchises will see fit to sign any more than the seven English players currently on their rosters – Stuart Broad turned them down in 2009 – is another question. As ever, with many of the current Aussie team sitting it out, the IPL's big battles come down to some of the big names of

Lasith Malinga: put all your Twenty20 money on Sri Lanka. But don't hold us responsible

Mitchell J: hot, hot, cold, cold, hot

yesteryear: Shane Warne's Rajasthan Royals (2008 champs) and Adam Gilchrist's Deccan Chargers (2009 champs) will be looking to set the pace again – and, let's not forget, this six-week burst may now be our only chance to see possibly the greatest T20 player in the world: genius fielder, maverick whacker and full-time fisherman, Sideshow Symonds.

ICC WORLD TWENTY20
When: April 30 to May 16
Where: West Indies

Already? Yep – just nine months on from the tournament in England, the world's top teams reconvene for the sequel in the West Indies. In fact, the World Twenty20 is scheduled to be a biennial tournament in the future, and this sudden follow-up is a welcome one-off. The first two tournaments have been, frankly, brilliant, with full stadiums and non-stop excitement on the park, English delight only boosted by Australia getting whacked by Zimbabwe (in 2007) and West Indies (in 2009) and English dismay only boosted by realizing we have invented yet another sport that everyone else plays better than us.

Bringing the party to the Caribbean should wipe out the painful memories

of the awful 2007 50-over World Cup.

What could possibly go wrong? Well, at press-time West Indies' top players were all on strike, leaving a team of unrecognizable rookies and veterans representing the Windies... that wouldn't be ideal.

England won their first-ever ODI series in the Windies in April and this is likely to be Freddie Flintoff's first big outing for England in the new one-day-specialist chapter of his career. SPIN's money is on Sri Lanka, though, whose none-more-varied attack (Murali, Malinga, Mendis, Mathews), ace fielding and innovative whacking took them to within a whisker of the 2009 title.

PAKISTAN v AUSTRALIA
When: July 5 to July 25
Where: In England, venues tbc

English cricket enters a new era as, for the first time, our grounds host a series between two overseas teams. Pakistan, unable to play at home because of security concerns, played a one-day series at "home" in Dubai in 2009. Now, they "host" Australia for two Tests and two Twenty20s on English grounds. It's a mouth-watering prospect: Pakistan's British-based

support turned out in noisy numbers for the ICC World Twenty20 last summer and will surely do so again for these games with the longtime world champions. For all the talent at their disposal, though, Pakistan's record against Australia is fairly hopeless: they haven't beaten them since 1995, and have lost their last nine Tests to the Aussies, including three by an innings.

Key man? Mitchell Johnson. Australia's all-conquering left-arm quick came unstuck on his first tour of England last summer, taking an embarrassing three Tests to get his radar right. He gets an early chance to make amends against a Pakistan top order likely to contain the usual quota of vulnerable rookies.

ENGLAND v AUSTRALIA ODIs
When: June 2010
Where: Cardiff, Old Trafford, Lord's, Rose Bowl, The Brit Oval

So soon? Yep, the international cricket cake just keeps getting richer and richer as cricket's top brass attempt to offer the public games they actually want to see. Imagine. For all England's long struggles with one-day cricket, their record v the Aussies is actually pretty good: it was honours even ahead of the 2005 Ashes, and even

Reigning champs Sussex Sharks (Luke Wright, above) will be favourites for the new-look Twenty20 Cup

after the 2006/07 thrashing, England managed to win the CB Series. That England success story was fired by Ed Joyce, Paul Nixon and Liam Plunkett. Who'll put money on any of them being involved in this series?

TWENTY20 CUP

When: From June 2010 onwards
Where: At a county ground near you

It's all change for the eighth year of the T20 – in 2010, there will be two groups of nine teams each (a North division and a South division) and counties will be allowed to play two overseas players (rather than the one they are allowed in the LV County Championship). The original mooting – when Sir Allen Stanford's cash was still in the mix – was for an all-star IPL-style affair with four overseas players, but that has been scaled down. Even

so, it's likely to be the highlight of the domestic season as ever and, with the carrot of a spot in the $6m Champions League, the one a lot of county chairmen really wouldn't mind winning…

ENGLAND v PAKISTAN

When: July 29 to August 30
Where: England

England play four Tests, five ODIs and two Twenty20s against Pakistan in the none-busier 2010 summer (the curtain-raiser to the summer is two Tests against Bangladesh). Last time out, it all ended in a none-messier diplomatic incident at the Brit Oval, as Umpire Darrell Hair accused Inzy and co of cheating. As a result of THAT, we can't even tell you what the score was in the two sides' last meeting: at the time, it was 3-0 to England, including Pakistan's deemed forfeiture; the ICC later amended the Oval result to a

draw, making the series officially 2-0; but the Wisden Almanack refuses to recognize the tweak and still has it at 3-0. So. Pakistan's heyday of three consecutive series wins in England (1987, 1992, 1996) is long gone but their bowling is certainly good enough to take 20 wickets – provided injuries, bans and the usual unforeseen circumstances allow them to put a first XI on the park. In the batting, Mo Yousuf is as immoveable as a particularly aggrieved prison rooftop protestor, likewise skipper Younus Khan. Do they have any others who can bat all day? Will they even need them?

40-OVER COUNTY LEAGUE

When: Every Sunday
Where: At a county ground near you

We thought it was all over for the 40-over Sunday League. But, despite its

Younus Khan: can bat all day. But not like this

Remember this? Not long to wait until the big return…

death notices being written at the start of 2009, by the end of the summer the ECB had unveiled their all-now county comp for 2010... the 40-over Sunday league. Hurrah!

When it was invented back in 1969, it was the Twenty20 of its day: the crowds flocked, the players were first sceptical and then bang up for it and the purists hated it because it was just too much fun. Then counties started playing Sunday league games under floodlights on Tuesday nights and the England set-up got sniffy about counties playing 40-over cricket when internationals were played over 50 overs. By July 2009, it was apparently dead. In August 2009 it was back, back, BACK, reborn for 2010 in a brand new, back-to-the-future format.

There will be three pools of seven teams – the "extra" teams will come from Ireland, Scotland, Netherlands or the Minor Counties. Teams will play each other home and away throughout the summer, with the tourney ending with semi-finals and a final in September.

The England team management are reportedly concerned that the abolition of the 50-over format will damage England's chances in one-day international cricket.

Why not just read that last sentence again until it makes any kind of sense?

THE ASHES
When: From November
Where: Australia

Andrew Strauss was on the open-top bus to celebrate England's 2005 Ashes win in 2005… and in the side 15 months later as they were absolutely hammered 5-0 in the return Down Under. So the England skipper, a

sensible fella, will hopefully have learned something about a) not resting on your laurels after a tight victory; b) not being over-reliant on injury-prone senior players; c) building a back-up squad of reliable pros, rather than promising rookies and d) having some proper warm-up games ahead of important Test series. Please.

Even so. England have not won an Ashes series in Oz since the Mike Gatting-Ian Botham-Chris Broad side of 1986/87. To do it this time would be a massive achievement. Australia's stellar batting will still be in place: Ricky Ponting will only be 35 and the almost-world-beating Phil Hughes will have had another 18 months to press his New Bradman claims. Plus, however indifferent Australia may supposedly be, beating them at home is never easy: England have won just five series in 21 tours Down Under since 1928.

QUIZ ANSWERS

OFF THE MARK

1 Tasmania 2 Trinidad & Tobago, Middlesex Crusaders, England, Stanford Superstars 3 Rob Key, Ian Bell, Jamie Dalrymple 4 Shane Warne 5 Captain of West Indies 6 He did not play any ODIs 7 Denesh Ramdin 8 Paul Collingwood 9 Kent 10 Anthony McGrath

NUMBERS

1 Graeme Hick 2 Paul Collingwood 3 James Hildreth

ENGLAND vAUSTRALIA

1 Ed Joyce, Mal Loye, Ian Bell, Andrew Strauss, Paul Collingwood, Andrew Flintoff, Jamie Dalrymple, Paul Nixon, Liam Plunkett, Sajid Mahmood, Monty Panesar 2 Chris Tremlett 3 Ricky Ponting 4 Peter Such and Phil Tufnell 5 Brett Lee

CURIOSITIES

1 Jason Krezja 2 Irfan Pathan 3 Eoin Morgan 4 John Crawley 5 Steve Harmison 6 Overs included eight balls rather than six, which has only been standard worldwide since 1980 7 Graeme Swann (v West Indies, Lord's, 2009) 8 Ravi Bopara 9 Dominic Cork 10 He was the first white man to play a Test for West Indies for 35 years

PICTURE ROUND

The grounds are
1 Kensington Oval, Barbados
2 SWALEC Stadium, Cardiff
3 County ground, Taunton
4 Newlands, Cape Town
5 Eden Gardens, Kolkata

TWENTY20

1 Kevin Pietersen, Andrew Flintoff, Dimitri Mascarenhas, Owais Shah, Ravi Bopara, Graham Napier, Paul

Collingwood 2 Worcestershire, Yorkshire, Derbyshire, Hampshire 3 Azhar Mahmood 4 Graham Napier 5 Steven Davies 6 Shaun Udal 7 Adam Gilchrist 8 Peter Willey 9 Darren Stevens 10 Chris Gayle

IN COMMON

1 They have all been overseas players for Durham 2 They have all captained champion teams in the Twenty20 Cup 3 They have all been contracted to Rajasthan Royals in the IPL

AGES

Nick Knight is the youngest (he is 40 on Nov 28 2009); then Shane Warne (40 on September 13 2009); then Mark Ramprakash (September 5 2009); Kylie is the oldest – she was 41 in May 2009

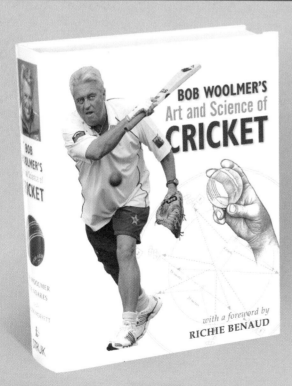